Volunteers & Redcoats Rebels & Raiders

A Military History of the Rebellions in Upper Canada

by
Mary Beacock Fryer

Toronto & Oxford
Dundurn Press
1987

in collaboration with
the Canadian War Museum
Canadian Museum of Civilization
National Museums of Canada
(Canadian War Museum Historical Publication No. 23)

Design and Production:Andy Tong
Printing and Binding: Gagné Printing Ltd., Louiseville, Quebec, Canada

The publisher wishes to acknowledge the generous assistance and ongoing support of **The Canada Council , The Book Publishing Industry Development Programme** of the **Department of Communications** and **The Ontario Arts Council.**

Care has been taken to trace the ownership of copyright material used in the text (including the illustrations). The author and publisher welcome any information enabling them to rectify any reference or credit in subsequent editions.

In the writing of this book the inferences drawn and the opinions expressed are those of the author herself, and the National Museums of Canada are in no way responsible for her reading or presentation of the facts as stated.

J. Kirk Howard, Publisher

Cataloguing in Publication Data

Fryer, Mary Beacock, 1929-
    Volunteers and redcoats, rebels and raiders

Co-published by the Canadian War Museum, Canadian Museum of Civilization
Bibliography: p.
Includes index.
ISBN 1-55002-024-2

1. Canada - History - Rebellion, 1837-1838. 2. Canada - History - Rebellion, 1837-1838 - Biography. 3. Canada - Military relations - United States. 4. United States - Military relations - Canada. I. Canadian War Museum. II. Title.

FC454.F79 1987   971.03'8   C87-094967-5
F1032.F79 1987

Dundurn Press Limited
1558 Queen Street East
Toronto, Canada
M4L 1E8

Dundurn Distribution
Athol Brose, School Hill,
Wargrave, Reading
England RG10 8DY

Canadian War Museum Historical Publications
Series editor: Fred Gaffen

Previous Titles in the Series

[1] *Canada and the First World War*, by John Swettenham. Canadian War Museum, Ottawa, 1968.Bilingual. OUT OF PRINT.
[2] *D-Day*, by John Swettenham. Canadian War Museum, Ottawa, 1969. Bilingual. OUT OF PRINT.
[3] *Canada and the First World War*, by John Swettenham. Based on the Fiftieth Anniversary Armistice Display at the Canadian War Museum. Ryerson, Toronto, 1969. Published in paperback. McGraw-Hill Ryerson, 1973. OUT OF PRINT.
[4] *Canadian Military Aircraft*, by J.A. Griffin. Queen's Printer, Ottawa. OUT OF PRINT.
5. *The Last War Drum: The North West Campaign of 1885*, by Desmond Morton. Hakkert, Toronto, 1972.
6. *The Evening of Chivalry*, by John Swettenham. National Museums of Canada, Ottawa, 1972. French edition available.
7. *Valiant Men: Canada's Victoria Cross and George Cross Winners*, ed. by John Swettenham. Hakkert, Toronto, 1973. OUT OF PRINT.
8. *Canada Invaded, 1775-1776*, by George Stanley. Hakkert, Toronto, 1973. French edition available.
9. *The Canadian General, Sir William Otter*, by Desmond Morton. Hakkert, Toronto, 1974. Bilingual.
10. *Silent Witnesses*, by John Swettenham and Herbert F. Wood. Hakkert, Toronto, 1974. French edition available.
11. *Broadcast from the Front: Canadian Radio Overseas in the Second World War*, by A.E. Powley. Hakkert, Toronto, 1975.
12. *Canada's Fighting Ships* , by K.R. Macpherson. Samuel Stevens Hakkert , Toronto, 1975.
13. *Canada's Nursing Sisters*, by G.W. L. Nicholson. Samuel Stevens Hakkert, Toronto, 1975. OUT OF PRINT.
14. *RCAF: Squadron Histories and Aircraft, 1924-1968*, by Samuel Kostenuk and John Griffin. Samuel Stevens Hakkert, Toronto, 1975. OUT OF PRINT.
15. *Canada's Guns: An Illustrated History of Artillery*, by Leslie W.C.S. Barnes. National Museums of Canada, Ottawa, 1979. French edition available.
16. *Military Uniforms in Canada 1665-1970*, by Jack L. Summers and René Chartrand, and illustrated by R.J. Marrion. National Museums of Canada, Ottawa, 1981. French edition available.
17. *Canada at Dieppe*, by T. Murray Hunter. Balmuir, Ottawa, 1982. French edition available.
18. *The War of 1812: Land Operations*, by George F. G. Stanley. Macmillan of Canada. Toronto, 1983. French edition available.
19. *1944: The Canadians in Normandy*, by Reginald H. Roy. Macmillan of Canada, Toronto, 1984, French edition available.
20. *Redcoats and Patriotes: The Rebellions in Lower Canada, 1837-38*, by Elinor Kyte Senior. Canada's Wings, Stittsville, Ontario, 1985. French edition available.
21. *Sam Hughes: The Public Career of a Controversial Canadian*, 1885-1916, by Ronald G. Haycock. Wilfrid Laurier University Press, Waterloo, Ontario, 1986.
22. *General Sir Arthur Currie: A Military Biography*, by A.M. J. Hyatt. University of Toronto Press, Toronto, 1987.

For further information on these titles, please write to the Canadian War Museum, Canadian Museum of Civilization, National Museums of Canada, Ottawa, Canada K1A 0M8

Introduction

Books specifically about the rebellions in Upper Canada are few. A classic secondary source is John C. Dent's *The Story of the Upper Canadian Rebellion*, published in 1885. Charles Lindsey's *The Life and Times of William Lyon Mackenzie*, which appeared in 1862, is less objective, for Lindsey was Mackenzie's son-in-law. These authors initiated the still widely accepted view that the rebellions were a necessary step towards the realization of responsible government, a conclusion that has been dubbed the Whig interpretation of Ontario history.

The most recent works are by two academics, Ronald J. Stagg and Colin Read. Professor Stagg's 1976 doctoral dissertation is entitled "The Yonge Street Rebellion of 1837; An Examination of the Social Background and Re-assessment of the Events." Professor Read's doctoral dissertation was published in 1982 as *The Rising in Western Upper Canada: The Duncombe Revolt and After*. Their combined work, *The Rebellion of 1837 in Upper Canada*, was brought out in 1985 by the Champlain Society. The introduction, which precedes more than 400 pages of documents, is an excellent recapitulation of the causes of the uprisings, the main events and their consequences. In a carefully balanced assessment they conclude that the rebellions had little to do with the achievement of responsible government.

The paucity of books does not imply a lack of other literature on the subject. Such writings abound in the form of articles published by historical societies, and as portions of larger works such as county histories. Because the risings lend colour to Ontario's past, they have attracted considerable attention. Thus relatively few primary sources remain unexplored.

What has been lacking was a study of the rebellions, and the border raids that followed them, from a military perspective. Militia records and material preserved in the British War Office have not been used as extensively as other sources. These records shed new light on the military history of Upper Canada.

In the initial absence of most of the British regular troops — professional soldiers who served in regiments of the line — the men of the Upper Canadian Militia shouldered the responsibility for quelling the risings. Afterwards, British troops moved into the province in substantial numbers because of the raids that were staged from border regions of the United States. To some extent the British government overreacted because of the separation of Texas from Mexico in 1836. Like Texas, Upper Canada had many American settlers, and the same pattern might be repeated. The home government overlooked the presence of many loyal settlers of British birth and other loyal elements in the province's mosaic. The British redcoats provided the pageantry and in some instances the steadiness. But citizen-soldiers of the militia in motley garb were usually the first on the scene to face invaders calling themselves by the highly inappropriate name "patriots". A much more fitting name is "republicans" since the only aim such marauders had in common was the severing of the British tie.

Acknowledgements

The Canadian War Museum and Dundurn Press wish to thank the following for their assistance: **Harry Bosveld**, Area Superintendent, Fort Malden National Historic Park, Amherstburg, Ontario; **Dennis Carter-Edwards,** Research Historian, Ontario Region, Parks Canada, Cornwall, Ontario; **René Chartrand**, Senior Advisor, Interpretation Division, National Historic Parks and Sites Branch, Ottawa, Ontario; **John Crosthwait,** Picture Curator, Baldwin Room, Metropolitan Toronto Public Library; **R.J. Dale**, Chief of Visitor Activities, Fort Wellington National Historic Park, Prescott, Ontario; **D.J. Delaney**, Area Superintendent, Fort Wellington National Historic Park, Prescott, Ontario; **Alan Douglas**, Curator, Hiram Walker Historical Museum, Windsor, Ontario; **Daniel Glenney**, Interpretation, Fort George National Historic Park, Niagara-on-the-Lake, Ontario; **J.K. Johnson**, Professor of History, Carleton University, Ottawa, Ontario; **Nicol G. W. Kingsmill**; **Ken Macpherson**, Picture Archivist, Public Archives of Ontario; **Rev. Michael Mann**, Windsor Castle, England; **Stephen Mecredy**, Historical Research Officer, Old Fort Henry, Kingston, Ontario; **L.F. Murray**, former Associate Director, Canadian War Museum, Ottawa, Ontario; **William Patterson**, Superintendent of Historic Sites, St. Lawrence Park Commission, Kingston, Ontario; **Ronald J. Stagg**, Professor of History, Ryerson Polytechnical Institute, Toronto, Ontario; **John Swettenham**, former Curator of Historical Resources, Canadian War Museum, Ottawa, Ontario.

TABLE OF CONTENTS

PART I
VOLUNTEERS

When Sir John Colborne asked him [Sir Francis Bond Head] *how many of the Troops, then in Upper Canada, he could spare for service in Lower Canada, he answered, ALL. . . The last detachment sent down was that from Penetanguishene, consisting of a Subaltern and thirty men. . . I urged His Excellency to keep it in the City... He answered "No, not a man!..."*

From *An Appeal to the People of the Late Province of Upper Canada* by James FitzGibbon. Montreal, 25 May 1847, p. 10.

The Parliament Buildings (1832-1893). The legislature was close to Government House and Upper Canada College.

Chapter 1
Emergency December 1837

The bell on the tower of Upper Canada College tolled the alarm. William Lyon Mackenzie's band of rebels was reported gathered at Montgomery's Tavern, on Yonge Street north of the capital. The following morning Lieutenant Governor Sir Francis Bond Head called for volunteers to defend Toronto. Among those who responded were boys from the college. Thomas R. Merritt, a boarder from St. Catharines, recalled:

We boys almost in a body visited Government House to offer our services to Sir Francis Bond Head to fight for our Queen and country. He received us kindly, thanked us, gave us each a piece of cake, and advised us to go home as soon as we could.

Upper Canada College (1831-1891). Many of the college boys went to Government House and volunteered to serve Queen and country.

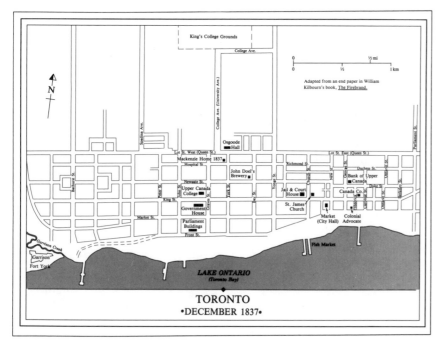

King's College Grounds

College Ave.

0   ½ mi
0   ½   1 km

Adapted from an end paper in William Kilbourn's book, The Firebrand.

N

College Ave. (University Ave.)

Spadina Ave.

Osgoode Hall

Lot St. West (Queen St.)   Lot St. East (Queen St.)

Mackenzie Home 1837

Hospital St.

John Doel's Brewery

Richmond St.

Bank of Upper Canada

Duchess St.

Newgate St.

Bathurst St.

Peter St.

Upper Canada College

Jail & Court House

Canada Co.

Duke St.

King St.

Church St.

Yonge St.

Jordan St.

St. James Church

Government House

Market (City Hall)

Colonial Advocate

Parliament Buildings

Market St.

Front St.

Garrison Creek

Fish Market

Garrison
Fort York

Parliament St.

LAKE ONTARIO
(Toronto Bay)

TORONTO
•DECEMBER 1837•

Thomas' elder brother, fifteen-year-old William Hamilton Merritt Jr., thought that the porter had rung the bell as "a lark". But very soon:

> The full force of the reality came upon us most startlingly . . . It was a curious sight to behold guards of civilians about Government House, the shops all closed, people hurrying silently in all directions, some with arms, and some without; then, at the Town Hall where was the chief assemblage, were cannon with torches ready to be lighted, arms were being distributed, and melancholy was exhibited in every countenance; nothing was done that day except various movements to defend the town, barricading the streets and filling houses with men; all was exciting, it was indeed a change agreeable from our dull work at College.

Thomas Merritt remembered the rest of their adventures that day. The two brothers and James Ingersoll, also from St. Catharines, "not quite satisfied with playing so tame a part, were determined that we would catch a sight of the rebels if possible." They ran north,

through woods (now Queen's Park) and cut east to Yonge Street, and saw nothing unusual until they neared the toll gate (above Bloor Street) where they caught glimpses of "rough men riding about, apparently much excited, one of whom galloped over to us and promptly took us prisoners, shutting us in the back of the room of the little toll gate house." They longed to return and report what they had witnessed, but one rebel aimed his rifle at a man who was running away, which unnerved the young prisoners.

About two hours later, emboldened, they worked at the window until it yielded. They dropped to the ground and crept on all fours to the nearest brushwood. Some horsemen gave chase, but the boys evaded them in the woods and fled back to the city much more quickly than they had left it. At the City Hall "the local organizers" were astonished at the safe return of the young adventurers, and relieved when they reported that the band of rebels at the toll gate was small. "We did not regret the rashness that had suddenly made us the little heroes of the hour."

Government House (1815-1860) as it looked in 1834. The lieutenant governor's residence stood on the southwest corner of King Street West at Simcoe Street.

10

The next day, 6 December, the two Merritts and James Ingersoll boarded a steamer which was going to Hamilton for men and supplies, and arrived the following morning. They drove to St. Catharines, which they did not reach until three o'clock on the morning of 8 December, owing to the bad state of the roads. There, the excited villagers were anxiously awaiting news, and "as we were the first to give the state of affairs in Toronto, and had actually been in the enemy's camp, [we] were again lionized." [1]

If the lieutenant governor rejected the services of what Mackenzie termed "Tory college boys", he welcomed the arrival of more mature volunteers. Sir Francis needed them for he had sent regular troops to Lower Canada, where rebellion had broken out in November. When Mackenzie's rebels were about to menace Toronto, Head had to depend on his militia, the citizen-soldiers, and again when Dr. Charles Duncombe's rebels converged on the village of Scotland, near Brantford, a few days later. Both disturbances were minor, but few Conservatives of the time doubted that had Mackenzie succeeded in occupying Toronto, other radicals would have joined him. Fast action by volunteers probably nipped in the bud what might have been a more serious insurrection. Yet Mackenzie drew little popular support. If he had succeeded in seizing the capital, his small force would not have held it long. Volunteers from around the province would have arrived to unseat the rebels.

In one sense the volunteers of 1837 and early 1838 did what the brave volunteers of 1812 were supposed to have done. Myth arising from the earlier conflict proclaimed that the Upper Canadian Militia stood shoulder to shoulder to save the province from American invaders. In truth, the trained British regulars were the ones who stood firm. The militia performed well, but the regulars provided the rallying point, the steadiness. One scholar, Dennis Duffy, saw the War of 1812 as a godsend, "an Easter Sunday that followed the Good Friday of the Revolutionary War". The sons and grandsons of the U.E. Loyalists who were resettled in Upper Canada after the American Revolution had to appear to be repaying the United States. [2]

At the time of Mackenzie's revolt, the distribution of seats in the Upper Canada assembly reflected a distrust of Reform goals. Despite some evidence of corruption in the election of 1836, the outcome seems two have been heavily influenced by Sir Francis Head's call to the electorate to support the Crown and reject "republicanism". Of the sixty-two seats in the legislature at the start of the thirteenth Parliament, forty-four were held by Conservatives, and only eighteen by Reformers. Since that election, which upset the Reform majority in the 1834 election, the lieutenant governor felt secure. Self-assured, Sir Francis Head felt he had no need of regular

Government House as it looked on 24 May 1854. The celebration was the occasion of Queen Victoria's birthday, and the artist was Lucius O'Brien whose father Edward was a militia commandeer at Shanty Bay.

Fort York at Toronto ca. 1845. The artist, thought to have been Owen Staples, was looking westwards from the city towards the fort.

Colonel Colley Lyons Lucas Foster, Commander of Forces in Upper Canada in 1837. Foster was fifty-nine years old when the rebellions began.

The military establishment at Penetanguishene as it looked in 1855. The garrison at the outset of the rebellions consisted of a lieutenant and half a company of the 24th Regiment.

troops, and he clung to a policy of depending on appointed magistrates throughout the province to keep order. As though to prove a point, when Sir John Colborne, the commander of forces in both Canadas, asked him to send what troops he could spare to Lower Canada, Head claimed that he dispatched all of them.

A War Office "return" (list) dated 1 October 1837 shows the strength and distribution of the regular force in Upper Canada. [3] Stationed at Toronto was the Assistant Adjutant-General Colonel Colley Lucas Foster, who had been commander of forces in the province since the close of the War of 1812. Most of the regulars belonged to the 24th (or the Warwickshire) Regiment of Foot. The regiment was below strength, with nineteen commissioned officers, thirty-one sergeants, and 421 rank and file. The commanding officer was Lieutenant-Colonel Charles Hughes. The term rank and file requires some explanation. It meant privates, obviously, but it also included junior non-commissioned officers, who lined up with them. Officers stood out in front; sergeants in the rear.

The Toronto garrison, housed for the most part in Fort York, had three companies, in all 239 rank and file, of the 24th Regiment. Additional members were Major Henry Dive Townshend, two captains, five subalterns, four staff officers, nine sergeants, and nine "trumpeters or drummers". Also at Toronto were seven Royal Artillerymen, and a captain and one subaltern from the Royal Engineers. The return does not show any Royal Sappers and Miners in Upper Canada in October 1837, but some were in the province later. When emergency demanded, officers of the Royal Engineers directed parties of regulars or militiamen, and civilian employees who worked as artificers.

At Kingston, where Thomas Fitzgerald was the town major, were three captains, five subalterns, one staff officer, nine sergeants and 150 rank and file, and one captain and five subalterns from the Royal Engineers. Four Royal Artillerymen were at Fort George, outside the town of Niagara (now Niagara-on-the-Lake). At the outpost at Penetanguishene were the fort's adjutant, James Keating, Lieutenant Frederick Chetwood, two sergeants and thirty men of the 24th Regiment. The headquarters for all these troops was Toronto, where the principal officers of the 24th were the paymaster, the adjutant, the quartermaster, and a surgeon. On staff at Kingston was the assistant surgeon.

Commanding all the regulars on the Rideau Canal was Captain (later Major) Daniel Bolton of the Royal Engineers. Under him were an additional captain and one subaltern of the Royal Engineers, and one company, described on the return as fifty-eight rank and file, of the 32nd (Cornwall) Regiment. Officers of the 32nd were one captain and two subalterns. Most of the 32nd

was at Montreal under the command of the regimental lieutenant-colonel, the Honourable John Maitland. Since the 32nd belonged to Montreal, the company on the Rideau canal was outside the jurisdiction of the Toronto headquarters. When Sir Francis Head declared that he sent all the regulars to Lower Canada, he meant only the 24th Regiment. The men of the 32nd, the Royal Engineers and Royal Artillery remained behind. [4]

The Upper Canadian Militia, in which the lieutenant governor placed his confidence, originated in 1788, before the province was created. That year, the governor in chief, Lord Dorchester, decided that the U.E. Loyalists who had been resettled west of the French

Tête de Pont Barracks at Kingston. Regulars and militia were both housed in this barracks during and after the rebellions.

seigneuries should have some local government. Until then the Loyalist settlements had been administered from Montreal. Dorchester established four new districts and gave them German names to please his Hanoverian monarch, King George III. The districts were Luneburg (the settlement along the St. Lawrence from Lancaster Township to the Gananoque River), Mecklenburg (from the Gananoque River to west of the Trent River), Nassau (the settlement on the Niagara Lake Erie). [5]

Each district was governed locally by appointed magistrates usually chosen from among half-pay officers from the disbanded Provincial Corps of the British Army, the official name for what are more popularly called Loyalist regiments. In addition to courts, each district was to have a militia battalion that could be called out in an emergency. All able-bodied men between the ages of sixteen and sixty were eligible, and by implication service was compulsory. [6]

When the first lieutenant governor of Upper Canada, John Graves Simcoe, arrived, he renamed the districts. Luneburg became the Eastern, Mecklenburg the Midland, Nassau the Home, and Hesse the Western. He also established nineteen counties, which were electoral ridings and militia divisions. At the second session of the legislature in 1793, the members passed the first Militia Act. The men were to provide their own clothing, arms and some ammunition, but Simcoe decided that the Macdonells of Glengarry County were to have broadswords from the government stores because they were adept at handling them. If called out in an emergency, the rest of the militia would be issued with muskets. By an amendment to the Militia Act, passed in 1794, militiamen were liable for service on lake vessels.

The system established by Simcoe remained in force, with certain modifications, until the outbreak of rebellion in 1837. At the outset of the War of 1812, Major-General Isaac Brock, Commander of Forces and Administrator of the Government of Upper Canada, was desperately short of troops. To supplement his meagre force of regulars, Brock authorised the formation of flank companies of volunteers for each militia battalion. These companies would receive more training, and serve as rallying points for the rest of the militia.[7] In calling for volunteers Brock set a precedent that would be followed during the rebellions.

Regiments in which all men liable for service were enrolled constituted the sedentary militia. This was a force on paper only. Obviously not every able-bodied man could be called out or the economy would suffer. Thus, in an emergency, the militia would assemble, and the commanding officer would ask for volunteers. Some volunteers could be formed into battalions of incorporated militia

Adapted from a map in Colin Read and Ronald J. Stagg's book, The Rebellion of 1837 in Upper Canada.

UPPER CANADA
•DISTRICTS AND COUNTIES IN DECEMBER 1837•

for specific terms of enlistment on what was called permanent duty, during which time they would receive fulltime pay. If an insufficient number volunteered, a commander of forces could resort to drafting, a measure not undertaken lightly for it was unpopular.

Members of the sedentary militia could also be embodied for short terms and paid for each day served. The main difference between "incorporated" and "embodied" militia was that incorporated implied permanent duty where a sustained effort was required. Embodied meant shorter length of service close to home. Incorporated militia could be moved about, to avoid boredom, or to relieve a unit that had been on particularly arduous service. Overseeing all the militia units was the Adjutant-General of Militia, with headquarters in Toronto. In 1837 that man was Colonel Nathaniel Coffin, who had held the post since the close of the War of 1812. Coffin was over seventy, in indifferent health and anxious to retire.

On the eve of the rebellions, the number of administrative districts had grown to thirteen through subdivision of the original four as the population increased. Each district had a seat with a court house, jail and municipal office. The following table shows the districts as of December 1837. Each contained one or more counties, while some comprised areas that were divided into counties later. Talbot was the newest, authorised in 1837, and the jail was still under construction when it was pressed into service to hold rebel prisoners. [8]

The militia units were still organised by counties, except for Gore, where the regimental lists were by district only. The population of Upper Canada by 1836 was between 370,000 and 400,000, and the sedentary militia, on paper, amounted to some 40,000 men. [9] After more than two decades of peacetime the militia

Name	Seat	Counties	Name	Seat	Counties
Eastern	Cornwall	Glengarry Stormont Dundas	Home	Toronto	York Simcoe
Johnstown	Brockville	Grenville Leeds	Gore	Hamilton	Wentworth Halton
Ottawa	Bytown (Ottawa)	Prescott Russell part of Carleton	Niagara	Niagara (Niagara-on-the-Lake)	Lincoln Welland part of Haldimand
Bathurst	Perth	Lanark part of Carleton	Talbot	Simcoe	Norfolk part of Haldimand
Midland	Kingston	Frontenac Lennox and Addington Hastings	London	London	Middlesex Oxford Huron
Prince Edward	Picton	Prince Edward	Western	Sandwich (Windsor)	Essex Kent part of Windsor
Newcastle	Cobourg	Northumberland Durham			

was in a neglected state. The regiments still mustered on 4 June, a precedent set close to the beginning. That date was the birthday, according to the new calendar, of George III, who reigned when the citizen-soldiers were first enrolled in 1788. (By the old calendar the King had been born on 24 May 1732. England adopted the new calendar in 1752.) By the 1830s the militia had become a ramshackle organisation, held together by a few enthusiasts who believed that the province needed to maintain some semblance of a force, or who enjoyed a taste of military life.

By December 1837 some militia units were in no condition to be called out. Officers' commissions were political appointments, resulting from having the right friends rather than competence. Thus in many parts of the province a cosy relationship existed between the militia, especially the officers, and the political party in power. Half-pay officers from the British Army and the Royal Navy were often given commissions in the militia, but often men with no military training were commissioned. Thus some militia officers were competent while others were incapable of discharging their duties. Also, in areas where settlement was recent, milita units had yet to be created.

Samuel Strickland, who, like his sisters Susanna Moodie and Catharine Parr Traill, wrote about life in Canada, explained how he joined the Peterborough Volunteers. On the evening of 4 December, a neighbour came to his farm in Douro Township and told him that troops were needed at Toronto. Samuel set out that night, in a snow storm, for Peterborough, and was joined by others along the way. They arrived on the morning of the 5th, and at what he called the rendezvous he enrolled on the spot.

> At this very time I held the commission of a lieutenant in the 2nd Regiment of Durham Militia; but as the distance from joining them at once, I thought it best in meantime to march with the volunteers. [10]

In areas where discontent was widespread many of the men, and even some officers, were Reformers and not considered reliable. All the militia units were poorly equipped. When Sir Francis Head called for volunteers to come to the aid of Toronto, officers led companies with names they chose themselves, names that were different from those of the old county battalions of the sedentary militia. When the militia turned out at this time, it was not in most cases in their regiments but rather as volunteers serving under any officers who would themselves turn out, and in other cases under magistrates. Letters and reports reveal how militia officers reacted to the crisis, but they tell very little about the average man in the ranks. Some of the letters sent to the Office of the Adjutant-General of Militia conjure up pictures of disobedient, careless, thieving, drunken brawlers. The actions of the few detracted from those of the majority. The typical militiaman, embodied or volunteer, was a small farmer, tradesman or craftsman who disapproved of, and suffered from, the destruction the rebellions created, and who felt duty-bound to help restore order.

Since 1837 was a time of economic depression, many enlisted for the pay and the issue of clothing. A private's lot was harsh. Pay tended to be in arrears, clothing in short supply, rations and accommodation poor, particularly in the early months when the government was taken by surprise by the risings. Certain petitions show that privates were often in straitened circumstances. Upon discharge they asked to be allowed to keep the clothing they had received, and for rations and travel money to sustain them on the journey back home.

Prior to each insurrection — Mackenzie's and Duncombe's — each leader raised an army of sorts, mainly of farmers whose politics were of a more radical hue than their neighbours who turned out for militia duty. Religion played an important part in determining who would rebel and who would remain loyal. Many radicals belonged to non-conformist sects. Notable among them were Quakers, despite their pacifism. Firm believers in the separation of church and state, they bitterly resented plans of the government to make the Church of England the established one and eligible for public funds. They were distressed that the province had so few schools, and they were committed to social justice. Some of the Children of Peace, a breakaway sect at Hope, in York County (now Sharon) marched to join Mackenzie. Quakers of Norwich Township, Oxford County, gave succour to Duncombe's followers.

All told, men willing to follow Mackenzie and Duncombe were few in number. When William Storey, who had been with Duncombe, was captured, he admitted that he had found plenty of "Captains and Colonels...but few Privates". [11]

Chapter 2

Background

O n the eve of the rebellions, Upper Canada was a largely undeveloped land. Roads were few, and better in winter than in summer. The best communication was by steamboats on the province's many navigable waterways, further facilitated by the opening of the Rideau and Grenville Canals to link Montreal with Lake Ontario and Erie and the completion of the first Welland Canal joining Lakes Ontario and Erie. Work had begun at Cornwall on the canals of the upper St. Lawrence. Railways were in the planning stage, and all large-scale projects were hampered because the province's financial resources were severely limited.

The populated areas were little more than a fringe along the St. Lawrence, Detroit and Niagara Rivers, and Lakes Ontario and Erie. Tentacles extended up the Ottawa Valley, from Lake Ontario towards the new community of Peterborough, above Lake Simcoe, and along the valleys of the Grand and Thames Rivers. Ninety percent of the population lived on farms, and the only places that could be called towns, outside of Toronto, which had a population of 12,000, were Kingston, Hamilton and London, although others were incorporated.

William Lyon Mackenzie, the instigator of rebellion, has been called the leader of the Reformers. He was the most vocal, but he was too intemperate to appeal to the majority of those who wanted a better form of government. He had emigrated from Dundee, Scotland, in 1820, coming first to York, moving to Dundas where he operated a general store, and to Queenston with his family in 1824. There he started his first newspaper, the *Colonial Advocate*, wherein he gave vent to his notions of what ailed the province. That November he moved his business to York. He popularized the name "Family Compact" for the ruling clique, and was almost hysterical in his criticisms of that group's public and private lives.

Mackenzie became a martyr to the cause of reform when in 1826 some Tory youths broke into his shop in York, destroyed his press and threw his type into the bay. He won a judgement against them that gave him the funds to reopen his press. Mackenzie was elected

Sir John Colborne (later Lord Seaton), commander of forces in both the Canadas during the rebellions and the border disturbances that followed them.

William Lyon Mackenzie.

to the assembly in 1828, 1830, and 1834. Between 1830 and 1834 he was ejected and re-elected three times. Mackenzie had enough popular support to be chosen the first mayor when York was incorporated in 1834 as the City of Toronto. A small man who sported a red wig on an oversized head, he became an advocate of American-style democracy. He was a rabble-rousing orator and an inveterate scribbler whose words, though not consistent, appealed to many farmers and poor labourers.[1]

The cause of the rebellions, briefly, was the control of government by a small group who dispensed patronage to friends, and who impeded development. A bitter bone of contention was the disposal of the Clergy Reserves, blocks of land set aside for the support of a Protestant clergy. The largely Anglican Family Compact interpreted this as being for the sole benefit of their church. The reform movement drew support from people who believed that the revenue from the sale of Clergy Reserve lands should not go to any church but be spent instead on education and internal improvements. The real cause of the rising lay with the Constitutional Act of 1791, which placed much of the power in the hands of appointed legislative and executive councils. These councils were not responsible to the elected members of the legislative assembly.

Myth shows Mackenzie and his rebels battling the Tory Family Compact. In fact, four definable factions may be discerned, factions that contained a variety of opinions within themselves. The radical Reformers were those who looked more to American style democracy for the answers to Upper Canada's ills. Among these radicals, Mackenzie, Duncombe and their followers, were those who would go furthest to achieve their goal. Also very active were the moderates led by men like Robert Baldwin and Marshall Spring Bidwell, whose demands for constitutional change, though equally unsettling to the Compact, were not as obviously influenced by American example. Some would serve in the militia, disturbed by Mackenzie's tactics.

Adherents of the Conservative group who supported the lieutenant governor were also divided into two factions. What may be called the high Tories were those who sided with the Family Compact, and they were probably a minority, as were Mackenzie's rebels. Behind the high Tories were the moderate Conservatives who were alarmed that the radical Reformers favoured republican principles that threatened the British connection. They believed that severing this tie would mean absorption into the United States. Many remembered the War of 1812, and were convinced that

Robert Baldwin, leader of the moderate Reformers. This portrait, dated 1845, was by Hoppner Francis Meyer.

Marshall Spring Bidwell, a moderate Reformer. Bidwell was defeated in the election of 1836. He left Upper Canada at the time of the rebellions and practised law in New York State.

without the support of the mother country, Upper Canada could easily be taken over by the Americans.

One example of a moderate Conservative who thought that way was Levius Peters Sherwood, a Judge of the Court of Queen's Bench, dismissed by Mackenzie as a member of the Family Compact. Sherwood's U.E. Loyalist father, who was born in Connecticut, the most democratic of the old Thirteen Colonies, was probably the first man to speak out for reform. The son, in 1812 a lawyer in Brockville, was the lieutenant-colonel of the 1st Regiment of Leeds Militia. Levius was absent when a party of Americans raided Brockville on 7 February 1813, and carried off fifty-two residents. He felt the responsibility deeply, and the experience turned him away from any sympathy with Reformers who harboured republican notions. He had no desire to live in a republic like the United States, where the multitude ruled.[2]

Government leaders and British officers tended to trust British-born residents, and to suspect people of American origin of disloyalty. Yet Mackenzie, the leader of the uprising, was a Scot. The American element was divided between the original U.E. Loyalist stock and the more recent arrivals, but British officers were suspicious of both groups. Certain U.E. Loyalist families were regarded as a loyal elite, the people who had stood for the unity of the British Empire during the American Revolution. From the latter grew the myths that U.E. Loyalist families were the Family

Compact, and that the areas where such families settled were the most loyal in 1837. Perhaps half the members of the Family Compact were U.E. Loyalists, but half were not, while the "Godfather" of the compact was a Scot, Archdeacon (later Bishop) John Strachan. In areas where U.E. Loyalists settled, other factors had influence. Such foundations alone did not provide the answers, for these families were not necessarily high Tories or even moderate Conservatives. Reaction to the movement for reform varied in different districts and depended to some extent on local conditions. Each district had its own oligarchy, which was not necessarily friendly to Toronto's Family Compact. When radicals rose in rebellion, the moderate Reformers were usually appalled.

In 1835 the Reform legislature had passed an act that made local government slightly more democratic. The act authorized the election of three commissioners in each township who took over the responsibility for roads and bridges, a task formerly handled by the appointed justices of the peace sitting in the Courts of Quarter Sessions. [3] However, the administration of the law remained in the hands of appointees chosen by the lieutenant governor on the advice of his appointed executive councillors.

Discontent with a form of government that denied elected representatives real power was weakest in the four most easterly districts. In the Eastern District many of the original U.E. Loyalists were of German or Scots Highlander origin. To these were added the Highlanders of Glengarry County, Macdonells who had been among the earliest to be evicted by their own chief in the infamous Highland Clearances. Families of German or Highland background tended to be apolitical. A British officer stationed at Cornwall to oversee canal construction was George Phillpotts. He was a captain in the Royal Engineers, although he was referred to as major in the records of the day. (The practice of allowing an officer a higher rank while serving abroad was a long-standing one. The higher "local rank" was sometimes a step towards a promotion, and as well it gave greater authority over militia officers who might challenge him.) Phillpotts informed Sir John Colborne that Roman Catholic Highlanders living in Glengarry County might make common cause with their French-speaking co-religionists in Lower Canada. His fears proved groundless. The men of Glengarry, with their traditions of warfare and military service, were eager to go east to help quell the rebellion in Lower Canada. [4] Besides, most were influenced by their own Bishop Alexander Macdonell, who was conservative, staunchly loyal and accepted by the Family Compact.

The Jones family, very visible in Toronto's Family Compact, belonged to the Johnstown District, but the Reformers were also strong there. U.E. Loyalist families, such as the Buells, who had Connecticut roots, were Reform leaders. Under Connecticut's

Spadina House, home of the Baldwin family. Spadina was built by William Warren Baldwin, father of Robert Baldwin.

Judge Levius Peters Sherwood of the Court of Queen's Bench. Mackenzie viewed Sherwood as a staunch member of the Family Compact because he was Jonas Jones' brother-in-law. In fact, Sherwood held moderate opinions.

Alexander Macdonell, the first Roman Catholic Bishop in Upper Canada. Bishop Macdonell exercised considerable influence over his flock around Kingston and in the Eastern District.

charter, all officials were elected by the freemen. To the Buells, appointed magistrates and a government not responsible to the governed were an anathema, yet insurrection was out of the question. Reform had to come through amending the constitution. The conservative faction was bolstered by many recent settlers who were Irish Protestants and members of the Orange Lodge. Ogle Robert Gowan, the first Grand Master of the Order in Upper Canada, had arrived in the Brockville area by 1830.

Long before Gowan came, Brockville had earned a reputation for feuding. The factions led by the Buells and the Joneses fought over politics, and over naming the town, which others called "Snarlingtown". Naming the community Brockville had settled that

quarrel, but the testiness remained. In fact, the fighting became much more physical with the arrival of Gowan, whose tactics of bullying far outdid the genteel fisticuffs of the Buells and Joneses. A detachment of regular soldiers would later be posted there, in part because of disputes between "the Militia and the political parties". [5]

In the Ottawa District, which with only 8,000 people was the smallest numerically, the factions were all conservative, involved in their own power struggle to control the local oligarchy. No one took much notice of developments in Toronto, which was too remote. Bathurst District had its two military settlements, Perth and Richmond, where residents were veterans of the Duke of Wellington's army and were ruled by their half-pay officers. Almost

Judge Jonas Jones of the Court of Queen's Bench. Educated at Dr. John Strachan's grammar school in Cornwall, Jones was considered a member of the Family Compact by Mackenzie.

Ogle R. Gowan, active militia commander during the border troubles of 1838. Gowan gloried in his role as the first Grand Master of the Loyal Orange Lodge in British North America.

as remote from Toronto as the Ottawa district, the people of Bathurst, too, tended to look inward.

The other quiet district was Prince Edward, with a strong element of apolitical families of German origin, and many Quakers. For some reason the latter were not as radical as the Quakers in York and Oxford Counties. Methodists, also strong in the district, were suspect for their church was too American. Yet little evidence has survived that many radicals dwelt in Prince Edward. Most of the Methodists were Reformers, but they were influenced by the Reverend Egerton Ryerson, the editor of the Methodist *Christian Guardian* in which he deplored Mackenzie's tactics.

In the Midland District, Kingston was generally loyal, but there were pockets of disaffected around Belleville and Napanee. These areas had been settled by U.E. Loyalists, but among their descendants the Clergy Reserves were an issue. [6] Newcastle District was loyal in the newly opened area around Peterborough, where some half-pay British officers had settled. Among them were Samuel Strickland and his brothers-in-law, John W.D. Moodie and Thomas Traill. Some disaffected people could be found in the older settlements close to Lake Ontario.

The Home District, which included the future counties of Ontario and Peel, was the most rebellious owing to Mackenzie's influence. At the same time, with some 70,000 inhabitants, it was the most populous, and it contained a substantial loyal element. Many of the farmers along Yonge Street were half-pay officers. Gore and Niagara Districts were divided, with strong loyal elements, but with enough potential rebels to have the authorities worried. Quaker farmers in Pelham Township, in the Niagara District, were well known for their radical views.

The other district with many potential rebels was London, where the proportion of American-born settlers was high, and where dwelt the other rebel leader, Dr. Charles Duncombe. The Talbot District had been separated from the London District only a few months before. The government believed that the new district had about the same proportion of loyal and radical residents as the London District. Yet the Norfolk Militia would respond well to the call for volunteers, and few in the Talbot District were destined to be arrested.

The Western District, like the easterly ones, was remote, and many people took less interest in the affairs of Toronto than in their local community. Some magistrates worried that the French-speaking people living along the Detroit River, whose settlement dated from 1749, might sympathise with their brothers in Lower Canada. Conservative by nature, the Francophones in the Western District were not destined to take an active part in the risings, although some were suspected of helping fleeing rebels to cross the border. Other residents were alarmed by the intimidating presence of Detroit, whose population had been growing of late. [7]

The greatest potential for rebellion appeared to lie in the Home District, in parts of Gore and Niagara, and in the London District. At the root of many problems lay the backward nature of the province and the lack of capital for development. The situation was further aggravated when an economic depression struck the whole continent at the close of 1836, followed by a poor harvest and inflation in 1837.[8] The bad economic conditions help explain why the risings took place at that particular time.

Regardless of location, four cultural groups showed the greatest potential for loyalty. One was the Orange Lodge, an offshoot of the lodge in Ireland that formed to suppress Roman Catholics. In Upper Canada, with such a small Roman Catholic population the members were dedicated to preserving the British connection. A second was the Indians, particularly the members of the Six Nations, the Iroquois, who had been resettled along the Grand River and the Bay of Quinte because of their alliance with Britain during the American Revolution. The third was the Black population, who saw in republicanism and the danger of annexation a return to the slavery in

View of Perth on the River Tay in 1835.

View of Kingston in 1846 from Fort Henry by W. H. Bartlett. Cedar Island, where the Cathcart martello tower was built, is in the centre of the picture.

the United States from which most had escaped.[9] The Roman Catholic minority, the fourth group, despite harassment from the more numerous Orangemen, was loath to be branded disloyal by its tormentors. Of the U.E. Loyalist descendants, an unidentified author, writing in May 1839, reported, "many have undoubtedly 'corrupted their way' yet the majority of them, there is reason to believe, continue stedfast [*sic*] in their allegiance." [10]

On 25 January 1837 Sir Francis Bond Head arrived in Upper Canada as the new lieutenant governor. He succeeded Lieutenant-General Sir John Colborne, a distinguished veteran of the Battle of Waterloo. Colborne had reached New York City on his journey home to England when he received orders to proceed to Lower Canada to take command of the forces in both provinces. The governor general, Lord Gosford, was not a military man and the situation in the lower province might require one. Writing of the Duncombe rising, Colin Read described Head thus:

View of King Street, Niagara (now Niagara-on-the-Lake), ca. 1854. In the foreground is the Niagara River, with Fort Mississauga visible on the extreme right.

A posturing, vainglorious individual devoid of political experience and common sense, forty-three-year-old Head proved to be the wrong man in the wrong place at the wrong time, for he was to collide violently with the demand for responsible government, a demand first advanced by various Reformers in the months prior to his arrival. [11]

Excuses have been put forth for the appointment of Head, a popular one being that he was chosen by mistake and that Colonial Secretary Lord Glenelg had intended to appoint Sir Francis' cousin, Sir Edmund Head. The home government was aware that Lower Canada was on the verge of armed insurrection, but entertained no such apprehensions for the upper province. The Colonial Office probably selected Sir Francis in the hope that a civilian might appease the dissenting factions. Sir Francis had had a short career in the army, but he was best known for his travels on horseback in South America that earned him the nickname "Galloping Head" and for his literary efforts, and as an administrator of the Poor Law. His instructions from Lord Glenelg were to be a conciliator, a role for which he was patently unsuitable.

Before long he had alienated people on both sides of the political stage. He showed himself a skilled campaigner in the 1836 election, by making the central issue that of loyalty, which brought in the Conservative majority. Afterwards, moderate Reformers such as Robert Baldwin went to ground. One supporter of the Family Compact who was disenchanted was William Hamilton Merritt Sr. To Head's successor, Sir George Arthur, Merritt wrote that Sir Francis did more to create "a feeling in favour of Responsible Government than all the essays written or speeches made on the subject." [12]

In a further effort at conciliation, Lord Glenelg ordered Head to appoint the former speaker of the legislature, Reformer Marshall Spring Bidwell, to the bench. Head refused, and on 10 September 1837 he sent in his resignation. [13] Some weeks had to elapse before a reply could arrive from Lord Glenelg, and meanwhile William Lyon Mackenzie began plotting to engineer a rebellion.

He took to the road, organizing political unions in York County, publishing a newspaper, the *Constitution*, and drafting a constitution on the American pattern. He deliberately deceived his followers in the country by claiming wide support in Toronto; in the city he insisted that the country was ready to rise. Political unions were

Sir Francis Bond Head, lieutenant governor of Upper Canada 1836-1838.

Louis-Joseph Papineau, who was the central character in the first rebellion in Lower Canada.

organized in other parts of the province, notably in the London District, some of which ended in disorder when gangs of loyal men, often Orangemen, arrived on the scene.

When in October, Sir Francis Head sent the 24th Regiment to Lower Canada, two men who worried over this move were James FitzGibbon and Richard Bonnycastle. FitzGibbon, remembered as the regular officer credited with winning the Battle of Beaver Dam in June 1813, was now a Toronto civil servant and colonel of one of the militia regiments. At the request of Sir John Colborne, FitzGibbon had been training a rifle corps of seventy young men to serve as officers in the militia. But FitzGibbon had begged Head to retain the detachment of the 24th that had been at Penetanguishene, which arrived in Toronto after the rest of the regiment had left. Sir Francis replied: "the doing so would destroy the whole morale of my policy; if the Militia cannot defend the Province, the sooner it is lost the better." [14]

Richard Bonnycastle was a major in the Royal Engineers and another veteran of the War of 1812. He had been in England on business during the summer of 1837, and he returned to Toronto on 30 August. Sir John Colborne appointed him Commanding Engineer in Upper Canada, and ordered him to Kingston at the same time as the regular troops were setting out for Montreal. Bonnycastle was to take command of the militia with the rank of colonel, as well as put the defences of Kingston in good repair. Kingston was the strongest defensive point in the province, and the depot for supplies coming from Montreal, supplies that might be needed to subdue the disaffected element. [15] Bonnycastle took inventory of the long-neglected, rusting arms, the ammunition that was inadequate, the moth-eaten bedding in the ordnance and quartermaster stores in Kingston.

While FitzGibbon fussed in Toronto, Mackenzie made his plans. He had been in communication with leading men among the radicals in Lower Canada, and hoped there would be a simultaneous rising in both colonies. The regulars, or most of them, had gone, and Mackenzie's men could make good use of the reported 6,000 "stand of arms" stored in the City Hall that were guarded by two constables. Toronto lay enticingly open to attack.

At Holland Landing, Samuel Lount, one of Mackenzie's staunchest supporters, began forging pikeheads in his blacksmith's shop. Pennsylvania-born Lount was a farmer, and surveyor's assistant besides keeping a tavern and a store in Whitchurch and West Gwillimbury Townships. Of Mackenzie's other lieutenants,

Jesse Lloyd, also from Pennsylvania, was of Quaker stock, and he had sold lots to found his own village of Lloydtown, in King Township. Silas Fletcher was a dedicated republican, proud of ancestors who had fought for the American Revolution in his native New Hampshire, who had land in Whitchurch and East Gwillimbury Townships. David Gibson, with a fine house in York Township north of Toronto, was a surveyor. Gibson had trained in his profession before emigrating from Scotland and he had received government contracts. Lount, Lloyd, Fletcher and Gibson were all men of substance who had prospered since settling in Upper Canada.

Mackenzie set the date for the attack on Toronto as 7 December, and he notified his two most experienced military leaders – Anthony Anderson of Lloydtown and Anthony Van Egmond of the Huron Tract. Apart from having served in the ranks during the War of 1812, little is known about Anderson's military background. Van Egmond was a veteran of the Battle of Waterloo with previous experience in the Dutch army. He had taken up land from the Canada Company, and had received contracts to work on the road through the settlements. His grievance arose over the monopoly the Canada Company exerted in his neighbourhood.

In the course of the first rising the military leaders on both sides were destined to be frustrated by their political superiors. Mackenzie refused to be guided by Van Egmond's advice. Sir Francis Head's treatment of his military subordinate, James FitzGibbon, was positively unkind.

Chapter 3
The Volunteers Arrive 4~6 December

I n the capital, all through November, apprehensive and excited, James FitzGibbon kept urging the lieutenant governor to take some precautions. Sir Francis, the chief justice the Honourable John Beverley Robinson, and most of the members of the executive council dismissed FitzGibbon as an alarmist. Two who shared his suspicions were the surveyor general, John Macaulay and Egerton Ryerson, the Methodist leader, who "pressed upon Sir Francis the propriety and importance of making some prudent provisions for the defence of the city, in case any party should be urged on in the madness of rebellion so far as to attack it."[1]

At the end of November a report reached Toronto that the Lower Canadian rebels had defeated British troops at St. Denis on the 27th. An even more disturbed FitzGibbon compiled a list of men living west of Yonge Street whom he could trust. He asked the mayor, George Gurnett, to make a similar list of loyal men east of Yonge. Their warning would be the ringing of the church bell. At that signal they should assemble at the City Hall (now the St. Lawrence Market). FitzGibbon would warn the men west of Yonge to assemble at the Parliament Buildings (on Front Street between Simcoe and John) upon the ringing of the bell at Upper Canada College, two blocks to the north. FitzGibbon showed a list of 126 names to the lieutenant governor. Sir Francis was angry at first, but he allowed FitzGibbon to proceed.

Next, FitzGibbon visited Chief Justice Robinson, who said he was "sorry to see you alarming the people in this way." Not wishing to offend Robinson, who could recommend patronage, the always financially troubled FitzGibbon agreed to warn only heads of families, not the younger men. He had time to warn only fifty before the insurrection began. [2] On Saturday 2 December, fearing that the disaffected might be inspired by the report from Lower Canada, several government officials met with Head at Government House. That day, FitzGibbon was in his office in the Parliament Buildings, where he received a visitor whom he identified only as "Mr. L.", who asked to speak in private. The visitor reported that a friend had

George Gurnett, mayor of Toronto in 1837. He first served as an alderman in 1835.

Chief Justice John Beverley Robinson (1829-1863). This sketch was taken from an oil portrait painted by British artist James Richmond in 1856.

James FitzGibbon, a contemporary portrait. FitzGibbon commanded the government force at the battle near Montgomery's Tavern.

seen bags in a blacksmith's shop containing what he thought were pikeheads, and long wooden handles were in plain view. FitzGibbon begged Mr. L. to come with him to Government House, but the man feared he would be assassinated by rebel neighbours if he were seen there.

FitzGibbon hurried to Government House, where he found Justice Robinson, Attorney General Christopher Hagerman, Solicitor General William Henry Draper, Speaker of the Assembly Allan MacNab, and Jonas Jones, Judge of Queen's Bench. On hearing FitzGibbon's report, Judge Jones, who regarded the public servant as a social inferior, "exclaimed most contemptuously 'Pugh! Pugh!' "

Sir Francis agreed to see Mr L. and FitzGibbon arranged to have

the man spirited to Government House. Still the officials and Head remained sceptical. The mysterious Mr L. could have been William Laughton, a magistrate at Holland Landing, and the pikeheads he reported, those that Samuel Lount made in his blacksmith's shop. [3]

Word of the meeting at Government House sparked rumours that Head had issued a warrant for Mackenzie's arrest. Since Mackenzie was in Stouffville, Dr John Rolph, whom Mackenzie intended making the head of a provisional government, advanced the date for the attack on Toronto to Monday 4 December, to preserve an element of surprise. Rolph sent William Edmondson from the city to inform Samuel Lount.

On Sunday, Mackenzie was coming south after travelling through several townships, circulating orders among his "officers"

Dr. John Rolph, one of the radical Reformers. Mackenzie expected Rolph to be the head of a provisional government when the rebellion had succeeded.

FitzGibbon took the copy to Robert Stanton, the Queen's Printer, but it would not be ready until Tuesday. In the minds of government officials, the security of the two local financial institutions — the Bank of Upper Canada and the Toronto branch of the Commerical Bank of the Midland District — was of prime importance. Two special units of bank guards were formed on Monday, each of thirty-five men. A total of eighty-one men served as bank guards, at the Commercial Bank until 17 December, at the Bank of Upper Canada (highly prized by the Family Compact) until 30 April 1838.[6]

At Montogmery's, Anthony Anderson, on whose military experience Mackenzie hoped to rely, arrived from Lloytdtown on 4 December, by which time 150 rebels had reached the tavern.

The market building in Toronto (1831-1849). At the time of the rebellions the market building served also as the City Hall.

to assemble at Montgomery's Tavern for the 7 December uprising. The tavern belonged to a supporter, John Montgomery, but he had rented it to a Tory, John Linfoot, who had taken possession of it on 1 December. [4] When Mackenzie reached the home of David Gibson, north of Montgomery's, he was furious with Rolph for changing the date. He could not alter the date again, for Lount was already out getting his recruits. At 7.00 that evening twenty men arrived at the tavern from Lloydtown, sent by Jesse Lloyd.

By 4 December, Sir Francis Head had changed his estimate of the situation. He summoned FitzGibbon and appointed him Acting Adjutant-General of Militia, to substitute for the ailing Colonel Nathaniel Coffin, and prepared a Militia General Order for the officers of militia regiments to call out their men:

Because of the advance in the date, the men lacked provisions and arms. Mackenzie and David Gibson went to Shepard's Mill at Lansing, on the west branch of the Don River above the Gibson house, to get ammunition made there. [7] Others were foraging for food. Later in the day Samuel Lount arrived with his recruits. At about 1.00 p.m. Mackenzie had a secret meeting with Dr. Rolph at a farmhouse, where Rolph recommended calling off the attack. Mackenzie refused, but agreed that the men gathered at Montgomery's were weary, and the attack must be postponed until they had food and arms. Instead four men —Mackenzie, Anderson, Joseph Shepard and Robert Smith — went to reconnoitre down Yonge Street.

In Toronto, a now very suspicious James FitzGibbon could not sleep, and he made the first of three visits to Government House. Sir Francis, who could sleep, was annoyed and went back to bed. Fearful of an attack on his house, FitzGibbon roused twenty of his friends for protection and they all went to the Parliament Buildings

for the night. An hour later a messenger reported that the rebels were at Montgomery's. FitzGibbon borrowed a horse and rode to the houses of some friends west of Yonge Street, asking them to go to the Parliament Buildings. Then he went to Government House, where Sir Francis was angrier than ever at being disturbed. FitzGibbon sent a law student, John Hilliard Cameron, to ring the bell at Upper Canada College. When Mayor Gurnett did not set the bell at St. James' Church ringing, FitzGibbon investigated, found the church locked, and sent a messenger for the key. To the toll of bells from college and church, FitzGibbon ordered the arms stored in the City Hall to be handed out to volunteers as they arrived. Next he rode up Yonge Street, accompanied by two law students, George Brock (a relative of Sir Isaac Brock) and William Bellingham, described by FitzGibbon as members of his rifle corps. [8]

They rode to 'Rosedale', the home of Sheriff William Botsford Jarvis, and seeing no one, FitzGibbon returned to organize the volunteers. Brock and Bellingham continued north and came upon

King Street East, Toronto, in 1841. This portion of the main commercial district lies between Yonge and Church Streets.

Death of Colonel Robert Moodie near Montgomery's Tavern as he sought to warn the lieutenant governor.

The escape of Alderman John Powell from Mackenzie and his friends. Powell brought the first firm news of the rebels to Sir Francis Bond Head.

Mackenzie, Anderson, Shepard and Smith, who took them prisoner. Meanwhile, Colonel Robert Moodie, a half-pay officer from Richmond Hill, had set out with some friends to warn Toronto. They encountered three lines of pickets at Montgomery's and rode past the first. Moodie fired warning shots; the fire was returned and Moodie fell, mortally wounded, and was carried into the tavern. Most of the others were made prisoner.

As FitzGibbon rode south, he met two horsemen — John Powell a city alderman, and Archibald MacDonell, the owner of a wharf on Front Street. Both men had heard rumours and had come to reconnoitre. FitzGibbon asked them to catch up with Brock and Bellingham. Instead, they, too, met Mackenzie and the others, who took them prisoner. Mackenzie had Anderson escort them to Montgomery's. Powell, who had two loaded pistols, lagged behind Anderson and shot him in the back of the neck, killing him instantly. Shepard fired on Powell and MacDonell as they wheeled and fled but he missed. They overtook Mackenzie and Smith. Powell fired his second pistol and Mackenzie's horse bolted. Powell galloped away, but Smith captured MacDonell. [9]

At Davenport Road, Powell abandoned the horse, fearing pursuit if he stayed on the road, and ran through fields and woods, arriving breathless at Government House. This time Sir Francis took the news to heart and began to dress. As Powell was leaving, FitzGibbon arrived, and a very agitated Head and some armed servants accompanied him to City Hall. There they found Chief Justice Robinson, Attorney General Hagerman and others. Judge Jones had already organized a detachment and left to guard the toll gate (south of Bloor Street) for the night. Sentries posted by FitzGibbon captured two horsemen suspected of being Mackenzie's messengers, who told him that Colonel Moodie had died. [10]

At dawn on Tuesday 5 December, FitzGibbon and Captain Frederick Halkett of the Coldstream Guards, aide-de-camp to Head, rode up Yonge Street until they could see the rebel encampment forming around Montgomery's Tavern. FitzGibbon hurried back to organize some 500 volunteers now milling about at City Hall and the Parliament Buildings. FitzGibbon wanted to attack at once, with a six-pounder gun, but Head insisted that he would not meet the rebels on their own ground. They must come to him.

To stall for time, Head decided to send a delegation of Reformers under a flag of truce to offer amnesty if the rebels would disperse. Several Reformers refused to go, but Robert Baldwin and Dr. Rolph agreed. The flag bearer was Hugh Carmichael, a

John Powell in later life. Born at Niagara in 1809, Powell was twenty-eight years of age at the time of his escape from Mackenzie.

While awaiting the return of the flag of truce, Mackenzie's force advanced as far as the toll gate (where the rebels captured the two Merritt boys and James Ingersoll). Each rebel sported a white armband, for identification, since the volunteers they might meet would not have uniforms. Mackenzie himself rode a white pony, and was muffled in several overcoats to protect him from bullets. [11]

When Baldwin and Rolph returned with Head's message withdrawing the offer of amnesty, Rolph had a private word with Mackenzie and urged him to attack at once. Afterwards, feeling vindictive, Mackenzie behaved more and more erratically. He had some men burn a nearby house belonging to Dr. Robert Horne, the manager of the Bank of Upper Canada, the butt of many of the fiery editor's criticisms. Some of his followers were disgusted by such vandalism and went home. Mackenzie also tried to burn the home of the sheriff. He was prevented from doing so by Lount and Gibson, whom Mackenzie had told that there would be no violence. Lount again had to step in when Mackenzie threatened to burn the house of J.S. Howard, postmaster of Toronto. At 6.00 p.m., with night upon them, the rebels finally agreed to advance. Lount's detachment marched three abreast, those with firearms in the lead, followed by

Home of Colonel Colley L.L. Foster in Toronto at Adelaide and Peter Streets. Foster boarded up the house to protect it from the rebels.

carpenter. Outside, the volunteers were boarding up public buildings such as the banks, Osgoode Hall, and the Canada Company office at King and Frederick Streets. At Montgomery's, with Anthony Anderson dead, Mackenzie prepared to advance on the city. Taking some sixty prisoners to make his force look larger, he planned two parallel detachments, one under himself, the other under Lount. In the end, both detachments went down Yonge Street, Lount's acting as the vanguard. At Gallows Hill (south of St. Clair Avenue) they met Head's flag of truce, and after hearing the offer of amnesty, Mackenzie and Lount had a whispered conference. Mackenzie demanded that Head put his offer in writing, and Baldwin and Rolph returned to the city. They found that Head had changed his mind over negotiating with the rebels.

pikemen, the rear brought up by those who had only sticks and cudgels.

In the city, against Head's orders, FitzGibbon placed a picket of twenty-seven men under Sheriff Jarvis on Yonge Street (in William Sharpe's vegetable garden close to Maitland Street). When informed, Head grudgingly let FitzGibbon leave the men there. FitzGibbon knew what he was about from past experience of night fighting. He remembered the confusion of the Battle of Stoney Creek in June 1813 when he was a lieutenant in the 49th Regiment. Men fired upon by unseen marksmen were almost certain to panic and bolt. [12]

When the rebels reached the picket, Jarvis' men opened fire, then took to their heels. Lount ordered the fire returned. The front ranks obeyed, and dropped to allow the ranks following a clear field. The men to the rear assumed that those in front had been killed, and they, too, ran away. Some paused to pick up two who had been wounded, and despite Mackenzie's frenzied pleas, they did not stop running until they reached the toll gate. Afterwards, refusing to fight in the dark, the rebels withdrew to Montgomery's Tavern and their encampment. Head ordered FitzGibbon to move the arms and ammunition from the City Hall to the Parliament Buildings, a safer place with open space around them where attackers could be spotted. FitzGibbon argued that he had no wagons, and in the dark there might be confusion. Before the argument was settled, Head's attention was distracted by the arrival of the steamer *Experiment* from Hamilton. Ashore stepped Speaker Allan MacNab from Dundurn Castle, the colonel of the 3rd Gore Regiment, with his horse, Sam Patch, and his fabled 'Sixty men of Gore.' Sir Francis Head, a great admirer of MacNab, who had brought the first reinforcement from a distance, decided either that the city was now safe, or else he forgot all about wanting the arms moved.

On Wednesday 6 December, FitzGibbon organised some volunteers and moved the arms to the Parliament Buildings. The lieutenant governor sent a message to Militia Colonel Edward O'Brien, an officer on half-pay at Shanty Bay near Lake Simcoe, to take some men he could trust and occupy the recently named community of Bond Head. That would prevent rebels in the neighbourhood joining their friends at Montgomery's. [13] There, a dazed Mackenzie was proving himself a man of words but of little action. His followers persuaded him to await the arrival of Anthony Van Egmond, who had not been informed of the change in date. Van Egmond, from the Huron Tract, would surely come by the 7th and would know what to do. [14] Meanwhile, some rebels drifted away from the approximately 1,000

Rebels marching down Yonge Street. This famous drawing by C.W. Jefferys was published in *The Picture Gallery of Canadian History.*

men who had gone to Montgomery's. Others who had set out to join Mackenzie, seeing volunteers marching from Simcoe County to aid Toronto, changed sides and followed them.

Colonel William Chisholm, the commander of the 2nd Gore Regiment, arrived by steamer from Oakville with volunteers from Trafalgar Township. Also on hand were Archibald McLean, a member of the legislature for Stormont, and Allan Maclean, the colonel of the 3rd East York (Scarborough) Regiment, who had arrived with 100 men. In Markham Township, Colonel John Button's son Francis began mustering his father's old cavalry unit. The men looked splendid in blue jackets faced buff and bearskin-trimmed hats. However, they would not reach Toronto until after the main engagement. More men came by steamer from Hamilton, while from Niagara the *Traveller* brought ninety-five volunteers led by Sheriff Alexander Hamilton.

At Erindale, the family home on the Credit River in Toronto Township, the sons of the Reverend James Magrath, Thomas and James Jr., set out with some dragoons who would form a useful independent company later on. The Magrath family had left Ireland to escape the turbulence of that land, and the sons were distressed at the prospect of similar violence in Upper Canada. Also with the volunteers was John A. Macdonald, the future prime minister. At that time a lawyer practising in Kingston, Macdonald was on a visit to the capital. [15]

Early on 6 December some 1,200 volunteers were in the city, the majority from the surrounding townships. The militia within the city was more diffident. Many remembered their first mayor with affection; others were worried that radical neighbours might attack them. In his office Colonel FitzGibbon was fretting because Sir Francis Head had not summoned him to prepare to attack. Then Attorney General Hagerman showed him a Militia General Order appointing Colonel Allan MacNab to command the militia in the district. Furthermore, FitzGibbon's name was appended to the order, although he had not drafted it, nor seen it before.

The affronted FitzGibbon resolved to confront Head at once, and before friendly witnesses he could trust. Accompanied by some of his supporters, among them Solicitor General Draper and Executive Councillor Allan, FitzGibbon found the lieutenant governor at Archdeacon Strachan's brick mansion on Front Street. After some evasions, Head admitted that he had chosen MacNab to command the attack the following day. FitzGibbon was taken aback and angrier than ever. MacNab's military experience was considerably

Judge Archibald McLean in later life. McLean and William Chisholm led the left wing when the government supporters marched up Yonge Street. At that time he was forty-six years of age.

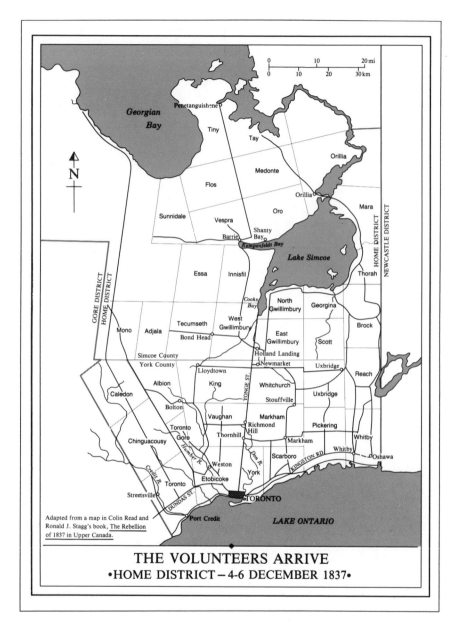

THE VOLUNTEERS ARRIVE
•HOME DISTRICT — 4-6 DECEMBER 1837•

Adapted from a map in Colin Read and Ronald J. Stagg's book, The Rebellion of 1837 in Upper Canada.

less than his own. [16]

Head had acted out of snobbery. FitzGibbon was an Irish nobody who had won his promotions in the regular army, to the rank of captain, in the field, rather than through purchase in the gentlemanly manner. Allan MacNab was the sort of man whose name would look well in Head's memoirs, a gentleman descended from the Dundurn cadet branch of clan MacNab. Sir Francis was equally impressed by the seventeenth chief of the clan, now the despotic laird of the Township of McNab, in the Ottawa Valley. The lieutenant governor would soon send The McNab, as the chief styled himself, a commission to raise a battalion of militia. Meanwhile, militia and only militia, would receive the important appointments for the attack on Mackenzie slated for 7 December. Although Captain Frederick Halkett would accompany the expedition, Head was choosing militia officers, among them Jonas Jones, as his aides-de-camp for the occasion. None of the other regulars still with the garrison would go. Colonel Colley Foster, barricading his house, would remain there. While FitzGibbon licked his wounds, Colonel MacNab ordered the arrest of a rebel sympathiser, Dr. Thomas Morrison, who was out making his rounds. A medical student who witnessed the arrest reported it to Dr. John Rolph. The student rode Rolph's horse to the western edge of Toronto and waited while Rolph followed on foot to avoid arousing suspicions. The following morning Rolph crossed the Niagara River and reached New York State. [17]

Chapter 4
Montgomery's Tavern and the Aftermath

T he many contemporary accounts of the events of Thursday 7 December 1837 contain a wealth of confusing detail. Sir Francis Head and James FitzGibbon wrote their versions, and both had ulterior motives. Head wanted to paint himself in the rosiest light; FitzGibbon sought recognition which he felt had eluded him. Lesser participants related their own impressions, often with no overview. Some thought that the rebels were dispersed at Gallows Hill, when they were about a mile farther north. Once the lieutenant-governor was convinced that the situation was serious, a great deal happened in a short time.

For safety, Head sent his family aboard a steamer in the harbour, and he passed the night of 6 December on a camp bed in the Parliament Buildings, where FitzGibbon also decided to sleep. FitzGibbon rose at 4.00 a.m. and woke Head up. The veteran soldier pointed out his eighteen years of military experience against MacNab's, as an ensign for only eight or ten months. Later, Head sent for FitzGibbon and told him that MacNab had agreed to step aside. FitzGibbon would command the attack. At that the Irish veteran rushed off to form his companies into battalions, and to select some officers. [1]

By noon his force was drawn up in front of Archdeacon Strachan's house in three columns, and an implausible organization they made. Few had uniforms. The rank and file included government officials, professional men like John A. Macdonald, labourers, and every able-bodied Black man in the city. Those who had horses, although going as infantry, were mounted.

Colonel Allan MacNab commanded the main column, about 600 to 700 men. Samuel Peters Jarvis, who was also the Superintendent of Indian Affairs, led the 200 men of the right (east) wing, while Colonel William Chisholm, assisted by Judge

Archdeacon Strachan's mansion which stood on Front Street West on the northwest corner of the present University Avenue. Government supporters formed up in front of the house for the march to Montgomery's Tavern.

Archibald McLean, was at the head of 120 men who comprised the left (west) wing. MacNab's column, with two 6-pounder cannon and provincial artillerymen under the command of Major Thomas Carfrae, a half-pay officer, would go up Yonge Street. Jarvis was to move northwards a short distance to the east, Chisholm by College Avenue and on side roads. All three columns would converge on Yonge Street south of Montgomery's Tavern. Three small troops of cavalry would go with MacNab, led by George Taylor Denison of Toronto, Thomas Magrath of Erindale, and Lieutenant-Colonel George Boulton who had arrived from Durham County that morning. Head, FitzGibbon and the latter's two sons, William and James Jr., rode near MacNab. As the column advanced to the martial

strains of two bands, enthusiastic crowds stood along the road. People waved from windows and rooftops, many with small flags. The day was fine, crisp and sunny. [2] Several hundred volunteers commanded by Judge James Buchanan Macaulay, assisted by Mayor George Gurnett, remained to protect the city.

Anthony Van Egmond reached Montgomery's Tavern at 8.00 o'clock that morning, by which time about 500 rebels remained, many still unarmed. After some disagreements, Mackenzie let Van Egmond create a diversion to draw off some of the volunteers, by sending Peter Matthews and sixty men to burn the bridge over the Don River. Matthews, apparently a reluctant, last-minute participant, managed to set fire to a tavern and some outbuildings near the bridge

Doel's Brewery Malt House, a place where Mackenzie's supporters met prior to the rebellion. The buildings stood on the northwest corner of Bay and Adelaide Streets in Toronto.

before his men were interrupted by the approach of George Ridout and some volunteers from the city who had seen the fires and were coming to put them out. The bridge remained intact; the diversion was a failure.

At about 1.00 p.m. scouts south of Montgomery's reported seeing the vanguard of MacNab's column. Mackenzie, still in his layers of overcoats, rode his white pony forward to investigate. On his return Van Egmond deployed the men. He put 150 of the best armed with Lount in woods half a mile south of the tavern, near the west side of the road. Another 60 he placed on the east side behind some rail fencing near the Paul Pry Inn, where a small force was sheltering, while, according to Mackenzie's version, some 200 who lacked arms remained at Montgomery's, where the prisoners were still being held.

MacNab's force now included Jarvis' right wing. After struggling over ploughed fields, Jarvis' men came to a stream and

Jeremiah Wilkes Dewson, who led some of the Simcoe County Militia to Toronto in December 1837. Dewson was quartermaster in the 15th Regiment, which had garrisoned Toronto before it was replaced by the 24th.

William Botsford Jarvis. A sheriff of the Home District, Jarvis commanded the picket that dispersed Mackenzie's rebels on the night of 5 December. His home, Rosedale, is commemorated in a fashionable Toronto neighbourhood.

Samuel Peters Jarvis, who commanded the right wing of the force that marched to Montgomery's Tavern. Afterwards Jarvis raised the incorporated regiment which he named the Queen's Rangers, in honour of the Queen's Rangers of the American Revolutionary War.

rather than get wet crossing it they headed for Yonge Street and joined the main column at Gallows Hill. [3] Of the left wing under Chisholm and McLean, little was recorded, although some versions claim that McLean and part of this column were the first to tangle with Lount's men on the west side of Yonge Street.

When MacNab's centre drew close to the brow of the hill (between Mount Pleasant Cemetery and Davisville Avenue), FitzGibbon had Major Carfrae bring the field pieces forward. The artillery fired round shot through the roof of the Paul Pry Inn, and the rebels escaped outside. MacNab's vanguard now rushed forward towards Montgomery's, some breaking off to pursue the rebels, who were fleeing from both sides of the road. The whole column advanced, the artillerymen bringing the guns closer to the rebel encampment. David Gibson was endeavouring to move the rebels' prisoners away from the tavern, so that the militia could not free them.

The artillery fired shots through the tavern roof, and some rebels rushed out. With the militia upon him, Gibson, to save himself, was

Thomas Carfrae, the commander of the artillery on 7 December at the battle near Montgomery's Tavern. Carfrae's uniform is that of a major in the provincial artillery.

Henry Sherwood, aide-de-camp to Sir Francis Head on 7 December. A son of Judge Levius Sherwood, Henry was later mayor of Toronto and for ten months in 1847-48 premier of the United Province of Canada.

George Taylor Denison II, who led part of the provincial cavalry at the battle near Montgomery's Tavern. He later organized cavalry, artillery and rifle units and was an active promoter of the militia.

forced to flee, abandoning his prisoners. Now the cavalrymen rode forward in an attempt to capture the fugitives, but many rebels eluded them because the horses had difficulty following through the woods.

The orderly column that had left Toronto had become a shambles. Despairing of restoring order, FitzGibbon galloped forward with Captain Halkett and others who were mounted, to look for Mackenzie. A rider spotted the rebel leader, but Mackenzie abandoned the white pony and ran into the woods. Unable to follow him, FitzGibbon gave up the chase and turned back for Montgomery's. [4]

George Percival Ridout, who led the force that dispersed Peter Matthews' rebels near the Don River bridge before the march to Montgomery's Tavern. Ridout was thirty years old in December 1837.

There, confusion reigned. MacNab noticed a man about to ride into the tavern, and he shouted, "Shoot me that man." Two of the volunteers took aim, but someone else shouted, "Don't fire! It's Judge Jones." [5] Had the order been carried out, MacNab would have been in trouble at home: Jonas Jones was his wife's uncle. Head ordered the tavern searched and burnt. Along with a collection of flags, the searchers found Mackenzie's famous carpetbag, which Head called "the Devil's snuff box", containing lists of names of his supposed supporters. This led to the detainment and interrogation of men who had not been involved in the rebellion on Yonge Street. Many on the lists had attended meetings or joined political unions, but had never contemplated taking up arms. After the excitement a witch hunt was inevitable, but for the moment that could wait. Head ordered a detachment of forty men to burn David Gibson's house, and turned the rest of his weary army homewards, as smoke curled from the wooden walls and roof of Montgomery's Tavern.

Riding south, FitzGibbon met the men making for the Gibson house. He disapproved but let them pass, since Head had given the order. Then Henry Sherwood — Judge Levius Sherwood's son a one of Head's aides-de-camp — arrived and told him the order was rescinded. When FitzGibbon caught up with Head, the lieutenant governor again changed his mind and ordered the Gibson house burnt. A militia field officer ordered to undertake the task refused, out of fear of reprisals, and FitzGibbon rode off to supervise the unsavoury work himself. He found the road almost impassable, for the macadamized part ended just north of Montgomery's now burning tavern. The house put to the torch, Mrs. Gibson and her four small children found shelter on a neighbouring farm that night. [6]

FitzGibbon reached home late in the evening. The temperature had plummeted, and he was "so stiff, cold and exhausted, that I could not dismount from my horse, and had to be helped off and supported into my house and laid down." When Chief Justice Robinson called the next morning, FitzGibbon asked him to convey his resignation to Head. The exertions of the past four days had left him ill. Besides, he was afraid that if he remained Acting Adjutant-General of Militia, Head might use him as a scapegoat if the home government disapproved of any action the lieutenant governor had taken. FitzGibbon wrote to Lord Glenelg himself, stating that he had burned the Gibson house on Head's order, lest he be blamed.

The rebellion had lasted scarcely twenty minutes, and casualties on both sides were light. Only one rebel, "Captain" Ludovick Wideman, had been killed in action. Others, who had been wounded, died later but the hospital kept no records. On the government side only five men had been wounded, none seriously. [7]

Head's next concern was the apprehension of the rebel ringleaders. He issued a proclamation offering a reward of £1,000 for the capture of Mackenzie, of £500 each for David Gibson, Jesse Lloyd and Silas Fletcher, men identified as Mackenzie's most influential supporters. Magistrates, small detachments from local militia, regiments, and volunteers without official status would hunt down rebels seeking to hide in the townships surrounding the city until they could find a way to escape to the United States.

Meanwhile, more volunteers were making for Toronto in response to Head's call. On 8 December Colonel Joseph Hill and Lieutenant-Colonel Jeremiah Wilkes Dewson began a march with 600 men of the Simcoe County Militia. The force was led by Highland pipers, and along the way, passing through Holland Landing, Davidtown and Newmarket; they captured sixty prisoners. These unfortunates were tied together in pairs along a rope for the march, and were later placed in the city jail. [8]

Urgent messages went out to militia commanders in the Niagara Peninsula, for the quickest route out of the province lay across the Niagara River. Even before 8 December, when news of the outcome of the skirmish on Yonge Street reached them, the colonels of the five regiments of the Lincoln County Militia had begun embodying their men. James Kerby, the collector of customs at Waterloo Ferry (upstream from Chippawa), and a resident of Bertie Township, was

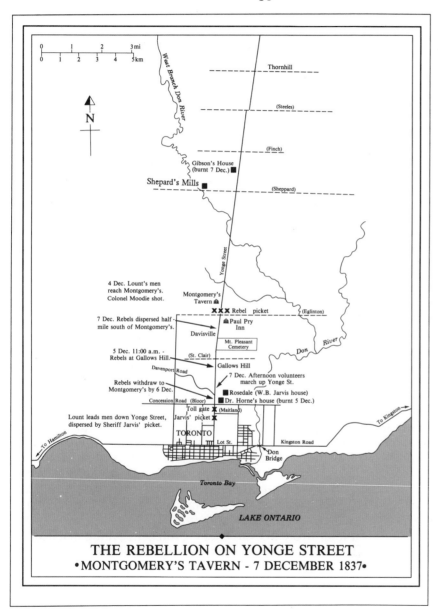

THE REBELLION ON YONGE STREET
•MONTGOMERY'S TAVERN - 7 DECEMBER 1837•

An interpretation of the "Battle of Montgomery's Farm". The original print is from Charles Lindsey's book on his father-in-law, Mackenzie.

42

David Gibson, one of Mackenzie's most active supporters. Following the battle at Montgomery's tavern, Sir Francis Head ordered Gibson's house burnt.

the commander of the 2nd Lincoln Regiment. On 6 December he had gone to his headquarters at Drummondville (now Niagara Falls) to plan the accommodation of his volunteers. By the 8th, his men were patrolling the roads and the river bank, well aware that Mackenzie, who had lived at Queenston, had friends in the area and would certainly come seeking their help to escape.

The dragoon company, led by Captain John McMicking, travelled the roads between Chippawa and Fort Erie, while infantrymen questioned anyone wanting to cross the river, and took oars from boats along the shore. In spite of these precautions, Mackenzie reached the home of Samuel McAfee, on the river bank opposite Grand Island, where he procured a boat. Once on the New

York side he proceeded on foot to Buffalo. [9] Later, Mackenzie wrote that before he left the McAfee house,

> One Colonel Kirby, the Custom House officer opposite Black Rock, and his troop of mounted dragoons in their green uniforms with their carbines ready, were so close upon me riding up by the bank of the river, that had I not then observed their approach they would have caught me at breakfast. [10]

Mackenzie's account suggests that the official militia uniforms were green, although very few of the rank and file had them. Dragoons, who were required to provide their own mounts, were usually affluent members of the community who could afford to pay for uniforms. Colonel William Chisholm of Oakville and his officers were described as having dark green uniforms. Chisholm returned to Oakville soon after the defeat at Montgomery's and brought a detachment of his 2nd Gore Regiment to the Niagara frontier to hunt for rebels. [11]

While Niagara seemed the most sensitive spot, militia units were being embodied all over the province. Before he sailed from Hamilton for Toronto on 5 December, Colonel Allan MacNab sent a message to Lieutenant-Colonel James Racey of the 1st Gore Regiment, whose home was at Mount Pleasant, outside Brantford. MacNab advised Racey of the emergency, possibly because he anticipated trouble in that area.

In the Huron Tract, Dr. William "Tiger" Dunlop raised an unofficial militia force that was given many names — the Invincibles, the Huron True Blues, the Huron Braves, and often the Bloody Useless. The men marched about the country, but were never paid, never saw any action, and were disbanded in March 1838. [12]

At Kingston the situation was very different. Colonel Richard Bonnycastle had made extensive preparations. Because Kingston was potentially another sensitive area, Sir John Colborne had sent Lieutenant-Colonel Thomas Cubitt of the Royal Artillery from Quebec City to command at Fort Henry, and he took with him a full company of men from his corps. [13] The two officers received the report on the outbreak north of Toronto when the steamer *Traveller* arrived on 8 December, with Head's orders to forward stores and to arm all loyal people and embody the militia. Within four days

Bonnycastle could brag that the lst and 2nd Frontenac Regiments had been called out, along with the lst and 2nd Addingtons.

Bonnycastle formed sailors in the vicinity into the Queen's Marine Artillery, led by half-pay officers from the Royal Navy and captains from steam vessels. The marines were uniformed in blue pilot-cloth frocks reaching to the knees, blue trousers, large fur caps, and equipped with belts and bayonets, pistols, light muskets, cutlasses, and for some, boarding pikes. Non-commissioned officers were distinguished by a white anchor on the sleeve, and Bonnycastle had four companies, or stations, of fifty men each. All were commanded by a navy lieutenant, James Harper, soon to be promoted to the army rank of major. The marines occupied blockhouses and lake batteries, the latter cold, miserable places.

The Frontenac Dragoons, under Captain T. Wilson, had provided themselves with blue uniforms faced buff, and bearskin-trimmed "helmets". The unit was eighty strong, with five officers. Ten dragoons were working as dispatch riders as far as Montreal. The Frontenac and Addington militiamen had been clothed at government expense in red shirts, mittens, strong boots with iron creepers, grey trousers, light grey army greatcoats and fur caps, and issued with bayonets, belts, cartridge pouches and muskets. Bonnycastle had hired two adjutants to train the men, and a garrison staff that included a quartermaster named Thomas Campbell, a former sergeant-major in the 79th Regiment and a Waterloo veteran with three medals. He had also hired a paymaster, surgeon, assistant surgeon, an orderly officer and a staff sergeant. [14]

Militia arrived at Kingston from Lanark, from Leeds and other parts of the Johnstown District, and from Prince Edward County, but Bonnycastle was obliged to send the men home for lack of space. As the depot, Kingston had the best stock of supplies, owing to Bonnycastle's efforts since October at bringing in the necessary materials from Montreal. The extent of his preparations indicated that like FitzGibbon, he knew that trouble was brewing. He had made good use of his resources, and had begun well before 8 December to prepare his militia.

At Cornwall, the concern was mainly with the rising in Lower Canada. Major George Phillpotts of the Royal Engineers reported to Sir John Colborne that the colonels commanding the four regiments of Glengarry Militia had assured him that their men were loyal. There were a few radicals around St. Andrews West, little more than a nuisance. The Indian agent at the St. Regis settlement, Captain Solomon Chesley, had informed Phillpotts that the Indians had lent their only field gun to the Cornwall Volunteers. After the rising on Yonge Street, Sir Francis Head gave orders that no militia should leave the province. Nevertheless, at Colborne's request, fifty volunteers, led by Colonel Philip VanKoughnett of the 2nd Stormont Regiment, had gone to Coteau-du-Lac to keep a line of communication open to Upper Canada. The Lower Canadian patriotes at Vaudreuil-Rigaud were in a position to cut the upper province off. These same patriotes, Phillpotts wrote, had threatened to destroy the farms of the Glengarry men if they entered Lower Canada, which had only made them the more determined. All they needed was Head's permission to march. Supplies destined for Kingston, to replace those being

The fort at Coteau-du-Lac, Lower Canada ca. 1819. A detachment of militia from Glengarry occupied the fort in December 1837 to prevent the Lower Canadian rebels from cutting the supply line to Upper Canada. The fort, now restored, is operated by Parks Canada.

Philip VanKoughnett ca. 1860 by the Montreal photographer Notman.

Lieutenant-Colonel Donald Aeneas MacDonell, of the Glengarry Militia. He was sometimes confused with Lieutenant-Colonel Donald Macdonell of the Greenfield branch of the clan who led Glengarries into Lower Canada.

forwarded to Toronto, Phillpotts added, would be sent from Montreal by way of Chateauguay, to bypass the patriotes of Vaudreuil. [15]

At Brockville on 23 October 1837, Ogle R. Gowan sent a list to Colborne of twenty men, his own name at the top, who were willing to serve wherever they were needed. They were eager to form a nucleus of a new regiment, the Brockville Invincibles. As the weeks went by, other units in the Johnstown District were preparing. On 16 November the 2nd Grenville Regiment mustered at Merrickville. The day was bitterly cold, but 660 men showed up for drill. All wanted to go to Lower Canada.

On 4 December a detachment of Brockville Invincibles went to Kingston. They returned on the steamer *Sir James Kempt* with Kingston's town major, Thomas FitzGerald, and a Mr. Leggatt of

the commissariat, bringing 800 stand of arms. The weapons were deposited in a stone building in Brockville, and the Invincibles stood guard over them for which they received neither pay nor clothing. On the 6th Gowan went to Perth, while D.S. McQueen went to Cornwall, with stores for the Lanark and Glengarry militia regiments. Gowan then toured the back townships and recruited 138 volunteers, in addition to those already enlisted.

A detachment from Prescott under Donald Murray and Dunham Jones went to Kingston and brought back a 9-pounder gun. All this activity occurred before news reached the eastern counties of the attack on Toronto. Until Mackenzie's abortive strike, the volunteers had anticipated going to Lower Canada. [16] Afterwards, they flowed into Kingston only to be sent home.

In response to Head's call for volunteers on 5 December, the militia of the Newcastle District (just east of the Home District) began organizing. Head's courier rode into Cobourg late that night, where officers met at the home of Sheriff Henry Ruttan, the colonel of the 3rd Northumberland Regiment. Also present were the Honourable Zacheus Burnham, a legislative councillor, and George S. Boulton, a member of the assembly for Durham. Burnham was the colonel of the 1st Northumberland, and Boulton of the 2nd Durham Regiment. On the morning of the 6th, some 2,000 men were ready to march, collected at various points. The 1st Durham Regiment was mustering under Colonel William Kingsmill, a former captain in the 66th Regiment. He had served on the Isle of Elba in 1815 when Napoleon escaped incarceration there. [17] The Newcastle volunteers began reaching Toronto by road on Sunday 10 December.

Loyal farmers along the Kingston Road in Scarborough cheered as 1,750 men of the Newcastle militia passed by. Near Gates' Inn, some volunteers broke into "Old King Cole", the song of the Cobourg Rifles, and the rest joined in. The inn's proprietor, Jonathan Gates, was a Reformer. Dr. James Hunter, a radical from Whitby, had sought shelter with Gates, and at the time lay concealed in a huge bake oven. [18]

In Toronto, Head had few places to put his volunteers, a cause of some discomfort and grumbling. The lieutenant governor sent out messengers to advise other volunteers to turn back. On the 7th, 400 well-armed men had set out from Peterborough for Cobourg, where some 1,000 others, including 170 Indians from Rice Lake, were waiting for the steamer *Traveller* to take them to Toronto. To their dismay the steamboat sailed past, but Head's courier rode in to inform them that they would not be needed. [19]

Adapted from a map in Colin Read and Ronald J. Stagg's book, The Rebellion of 1837 in Upper Canada.

NEWCASTLE AND MIDLAND DISTRICTS
•1838•

Chapter 5
Rebellion in the London District

In the Home District the hunt was on for rebels and sympathizers known to be still in the neighbourhood, and many suspects were arrested. The jail at Toronto was overflowing, and prisoners were being confined in the City Hall and other public buildings. Yet even as Sir Francis Head was writing to Lord Glenelg to inform him that the revolt had been crushed, another insurrection was about to burst forth in the London District. Contrary to opinion at the time and since, this was a separate outbreak and not necessarily co-ordinated with Mackenzie's. There had been contact between the leaders in the London District and Mackenzie, but no overall plan to act in concert. However, the actual rising was precipitated by the rumour on 7 December that Mackenzie had taken Toronto. Rebels from sixteen townships were involved, fourteen in the London District, and two adjacent ones — Dumfries and Brantford Townships — in the Gore District. [1]

As in the Home District there had been meetings to form political unions. Then, on 6 December, George Washington Case of Hamilton arrived in the townships of Burford and Oakland, on the east side of the London District. Case reported that Mackenzie's men were gathering north of Toronto and the local sheriff intended to arrest Dr. Charles Duncombe and one of the Malcolms. Duncombe sent letters to his supporters and suggested a meeting at Sodom village, in Norwich Township. The letters on the way, Duncombe left his home in Bishopsgate, Burford Township, and rode to Sodom. Duncombe had been born in Connecticut and

raised in New York. A medical doctor, he settled in the district in 1819. He had been a member of the legislature representing Oxford County since 1834, and was one of the sixteen Reformers who had survived the Conservative sweep in 1836. He was also a close associate of Dr. John Rolph, the member for Norfolk County who had fled before the rising on Yonge Street. [2]

The Malcolm whom Case mentioned was probably Eliakim, a

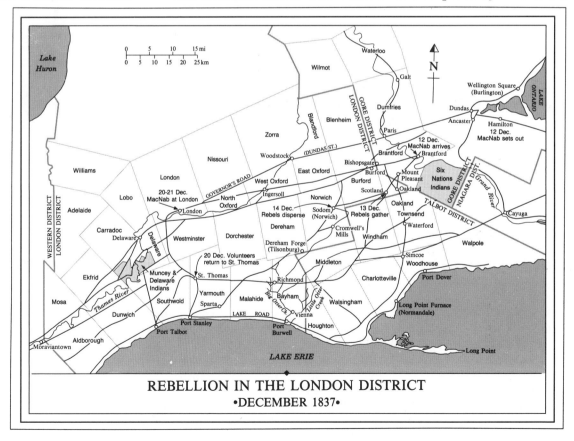

REBELLION IN THE LONDON DISTRICT
•DECEMBER 1837•

Dr. Charles Duncombe, one of two leaders of the rebellion in the London District. Duncombe's name was to be given to the rising.

Eliakim Malcolm, leader of the rebels around Scotland, near Brantford. The picture is reproduced from F. Douglas Reville's book on Brant County.

leader of dissent in Oakland Township, where he owned a thousand acres of land. The first Malcolm had been a U.E. Loyalist from Maine who brought his family to New Brunswick and, in 1795, to Oakland. His sons and grandsons were nearly all radicals, possibly because they resented that they were only partly compensated for damage to their properties during the War of 1812. Duncombe became known as the instigator of the rising, but Malcolm was as active and the more aggressive of the two. [3]

Norwich Township in Oxford County, was well known for its radical Quakers, but others were found in Yarmouth Township, Middlesex County. At Sparta in Yarmouth, Quaker Joshua Doan raised a rebel band known as Doan's Spartan Rangers.[4] There were also other areas of dissent in the district and additional

rebel leaders

On 8 or 9 December — the exact date is uncertain — Duncombe addressed the Norwich meeting at Sodom, warning his audience that the government was about to arrest many Reformers. Eighty men enlisted, and in several townships others began drilling. Their objective would be Brantford, and then Hamilton, where a radical John G. Parker, had been jailed. After dealing with the Tories in the Brantford area, the radicals intended freeing Parker.

Brantford had already been alerted, not only by MacNab's message of 5 December to Lieutenant-Colonel James Racey, but by the arrival of a courier from Head. By the 7th, part of the 1st Gore Regiment, raised in Ancaster and the adjacent Indian lands, had assembled at Brantford. (The militia of Brantford Township apparently was not called out as the men were not considered reliable.) On the 8th, Racey wrote to Colonel Coffin, the ailing Adjutant-General of Militia, that he would send him information on the activities of the radicals in the nearby townships. [5]

By 10 December, Colonel MacNab was back in Hamilton after leading the central column up Yonge Street. Earlier that day his subordinate in the 3rd Gore Regiment, Lieutenant-Colonel Robert Land, had received a visit from Charles Strange Perley of Burford. Perley reported that Duncombe had raised between 100 and 200 men in Norwich, while Eliakim Malcolm had some 60 men at the village of Scotland, in Oakland Township. [6] MacNab already had orders from Head to march into the London District with 500 volunteers in case of trouble there.

During MacNab's absence in Toronto, Lieutenant-Colonel Land had been embodying the 3rd Gore Regiment, drawn from Hamilton and Barton Township, and other volunteers had arrived. In Guelph, anticipating that men would be needed to guard the Niagara frontier, Captain John Poore had embodied sixty-two men as the Guelph Rifles. Poore's force reached Dundas on the 7th. That village was a nest of radicals, and during the night some threw stones at Bamberger's Hotel, where the volunteers were sleeping. The following day the Guelph men marched on to Hamilton and were accommodated in the court house. On 12 December, when MacNab left town with 300 volunteers, Poore and his riflemen were among them. [7]

Loyal men in the townships along Lake Erie were becoming

Dundurn Castle, home of Colonel Allan MacNab at Hamilton, Ontario. MacNab rode forth on Christmas Day 1837 with volunteers for the Niagara frontier. The castle, maintained by the City of Hamilton, is open to the public.

Colonel Allan MacNab of Dundurn, commander of the expedition against the rebels in the London District, ca. 1854. MacNab was knighted although the British government disapproved of the destruction of the American steamer *Caroline*.

aware of preparations in their neighbourhoods, and in Burford and Oakland. At Port Burwell, in Bayham township, John Burwell, a magistrate, wrote to John Joseph, the lieutenant governor's secretary, urging that the local militia be embodied at once, and offering his services to the government. [8] In Malahide Township, Magistrate Doyle McKenny raised a party of volunteers and hoped to intercept some rebels making for Scotland, where they were to assemble. Led by David Anderson, the rebels marched from Yarmouth, taking some supply wagons, and adding to their numbers as they passed through Malahide and Bayham Townships. They crossed the bridge over Big Otter Creek on the evening of 12

December, before the volunteers reached that spot.

In several townships, militia officers were embodying individual companies. John Burwell had his in Bayham, and like McKenny he tried to intercept Anderson's men but without success, this time on the Talbot Road. Anderson reached Oakland on Wednesday 13 December. [9] In Malahide, Captain Henry Medcalf and his company also failed to stop any rebels marching for Oakland. The St. Thomas volunteers, both cavalry and infantry, were making ready. In Simcoe, on hearing that eighty rebels were north of Waterford, half way to Oakland, the militia turned out to march to Round Plains, northwest of Waterford, to await instructions from Brantford.

By 13 December, Duncombe's men from Norwich and Burford, and Malcolm's from Oakland, with some insurgents from as far west as Yarmouth and Dereham Townships, were gathered at Scotland. Estimates vary but the probable number was 400. Of interest, if not importance, was the presence of thirty-three-year-old Samuel Edison, an innkeeper from Vienna, in Bayham, and a lieutenant in the rebel force. Edison had probably been recruited by Eliakim Malcolm's nephew, Finlay Malcolm, a resident of Bayham who led some rebels to Oakland. [10] (Edison escaped to the United States. His famous inventor son Thomas was born at Milan, Ohio, in 1847.) At Scotland, the rebels received word that Mackenzie had been put to flight, information that had reached London four days earlier, on the 9th. Then the axe fell. A horseman brought word that MacNab was in Brantford with his volunteers, the force from Hamilton had been augmented by 150 men of the 1st Gore Regiment and 100 Indians from the Six Nations lands on the Grand River. After some discussion, during which Eliakim Malcolm suggested attacking Simcoe, Duncombe resolved to withdraw into Norwich. Rumour suggested that MacNab would advance on Scotland with some cannon, and in Norwich they would be safer. Augustus Chaple, an insurgent captured later, stated that, with the road so bad, "Cannon could not git there." [11]

At Brantford, at 9.00 o'clock on the morning of the 13th, MacNab received a report that Duncombe was preparing to withdraw from Scotland. MacNab dispatched couriers to London, Woodstock and Simcoe asking the militia officers to raise volunteers and come towards Scotland. With his Hamilton and Brantford militia, the Indians, and some cavalry probably from Brantford, MacNab left for Scotland at 1.00 a.m. on Tuesday 14 December, a distance of some twelve miles. As he drew near he divided his force. Two roads led into the village from the east, and these his troops took.

The Indians swung round and approached from the northwest, where there was no road. With Scotland outflanked the cavalry cantered ahead and entered the settlement.

Duncombe had left some sentries behind, and these opened fire on the riders, hitting an officer's horse. Hopelessly outnumbered the few rebels ran away, apparently pursued by Indians, which gave rise to the ugly story that three of the sentries were shot and then scalped. Such an event was most unlikely in Upper Canada in 1837, but just what the Americans, beginning to take an interest in the unrest north of the border, wanted to hear. A letter describing the atrocity appeared in the Rochester *Democrat* dated 17 December. However, none of the rebels or their families referred to any Indian atrocities at Scotland. Furthermore, Sir Francis Head informed William Johnson Kerr of Wellington Square (Burlington) that the behaviour of the Indians had been "humane and steady." [12] Kerr, who was part Mohawk, was the Indian agent for the Grand River community.

Within hours the volunteers from the London District began arriving at Scotland. The first were 160 men from Simcoe. That afternoon 167 men from Yarmouth came in, after a march of some 60 miles in twenty-three hours. They had been raised by John B. Askin, the major of the 3rd Middlesex Regiment, who had received permission from his colonel, John Bostwick, a resident of Port Stanley. The men of Bostwick's militia regiment were drawn from the townships of Westminster, Dorchester and Delaware as well as Yarmouth. Askin had had them on the march before MacNab's message reached London. When he heard of insurgents gathering at Scotland, Askin had taken the initiative.

Later in the day, three men came as a delegation from Norwich to ask MacNab whether the rebels might be granted an amnesty. Two versions of MacNab's reply were recorded. Solomon Lossing, a justice of the peace, mill owner and former Quaker, was one of the delegation, although he had not been with the rebels at Scotland. Lossing claimed that MacNab promised to intercede for any who surrendered. In a letter to Captain Frederick Halkett, Head's aide-de-camp, MacNab maintained that he told Lossing he could not promise pardons until the rebel leaders had been handed over to him. [13]

MacNab set out for Norwich in pursuit of the rebels, a march likened almost, in reports published in American newspapers, to that of Attila the Hun. If MacNab was high-handed, he had reason. Arrangements for his expedition had been makeshift and hasty from the outset. His men had to have places to sleep, and in obtaining billets he was arbitrary. He had to order home owners to take in his troops and to feed them. In the interest of speed his men had travelled light and he had neither a commissariat officer nor enough supplies to sustain a force that now numbered more than 800 men. Officers were supposed to hand out receipts for which payment could be made by the district treasurer, an unusual procedure. [14]

View of London, Upper Canada, ca. 1842. The artist was John Herbert (1801-1887).The substantial courthouse is the highest building on the horizon.

51

Such receipts were rarely honoured afterwards.

Under normal circumstances, where regulars were on the move, expenses were met from a military chest. Regular officers were meticulous at filing their accounts. Deficiencies had to be made up from their own pockets, and they knew to produce proof for all their purchases. Record keeping during the two rebellions was otherwise generally poor. Head did not issue instructions for accurate accountings, and in the excitement few militia officers paid any attention to the cost of operations. As a consequence many people who helped supply MacNab's army were never paid at all, and some who were eventually compensated had to wait years. [15]

Once the rebels in Norwich realized that MacNab was coming, they again dispersed, but militia were converging from all sides to intercept fugitives. A force of sixty Woodstock men commanded by

Lieutenant-Colonel Peter Boyle de Blaquiere of the 3rd Oxford Regiment had linked up with fifty Ingersoll volunteers led by Captain William Rothwell. By 15 December this force was northwest of Sodom, attempting to cut off rebels escaping in that direction.

On the 16th, at Sodom, MacNab received 103 residents of Norwich who brought a petition. They claimed that they had no real grievances, and had been led astray by their unscrupulous leaders. They asked MacNab to see if he could persuade the lieutenant governor to pardon them. If so, they promised to remain peaceful and to do what they could to have the ringleaders captured. Solomon Lossing, of the previous delegation, was with them, and MacNab arrested him on the grounds that he had supplied food to the rebels. MacNab let most of the others return to their homes, but they might have to surrender if Sir Francis Head did not approve. He detained a few of those suspected of having given leadership for transport to jail in London. [16]

MacNab was taking the initiative, unaware of an order dated 10 December from Head specifying that militia officers, regardless of rank, could not free prisoners. Then on the 14th the lieutenant governor changed his mind and he issued a proclamation which allowed MacNab the very latitude he had been taking. Only the most "notorious" rebels were to be arrested by the militia, and where a local magistrate would issue a warrant. [17]

MacNab remained at Sodom until 19 December while his men scoured the area. The volunteers disarmed all those suspected of holding rebel sympathies, and arrested anyone who might have been involved with Charles Duncombe, Eliakim Malcolm or lesser ringleaders. Writing to Judge Jonas Jones on the 18th, MacNab reported having taken 500 prisoners and some 100 to 200 rifles. His letter was published as an *Extra* to the Hamilton *Gazette* on 2 January 1838. [18] While MacNab was at Sodom, other militia units were searching the fourteen rebellious townships in the London District and

The cemetery in Vienna, Ontario, where Thomas Edison's wife is buried. Samuel Edison, the famous inventor's father, fled to the United States after taking part in the rising, but Thomas was a frequent visitor at the farm of his grandparents nearby.

Brantford and Dumfries in Gore District.

At Galt, Absalom Shade (an employee of William Dickson, the founder of the village and the colonel of the 4th Gore Regiment) organized a company but it was not used. Instead a company was sent to Galt from Fergus to guard the bridge over the Grand River and watch for fleeing rebels. Militia from Cayuga went to block the route eastwards. Volunteers from St. Thomas led by John B. Askin set off on the 18th for the rebellious Lake Erie townships. They swept through Dereham, and on to Bayham, Malahide and Yarmouth, returning to St. Thomas on the 20th with some thirty-eight prisoners who would be sent to London.

For many inhabitants, the very mention that Indians were on the way was enough to strike terror in their hearts. In Dorchester Township some Reformers decided to band together for protection, while those in Delaware feared that the government might use Delaware and Muncey Indians against them, for the reserve was close by. The latter formed a political union for self defence. [19]

When MacNab was about to leave Norwich on the 19th, he allowed some of the men from Hamilton who had been with him from the beginning to return to their homes. He intended marching on to London, but 150 to 200 reinforcements were on their way from Hamilton to join him. These included a fledgling company of eighteen Blacks under a white officer, Captain William Allen. This was the first "coloured" company, but others would be formed as time passed. [20]

MacNab made a fast march to London, while detachments of his men escorted prisoners there. He left scant records of how his soldiers travelled. Those with horses were mounted. Others may have been on foot, or in wagons if the roads were passable. He planned to leave volunteer units of from 100 to 150 men each in London, Woodstock, Simcoe and Brantford, but no record suggests that he did so. Certainly part of the militia in the district remained embodied for some days. Sir Francis feared more trouble there, but a satisfied MacNab was back in Hamilton with some of his men by Christmas Eve. [21] In the London District, as in the Toronto rising, volunteers from the various militia units, but serving independently of them, could write with pride of the response of the loyal inhabitants. Volunteers had been the key to success.

In Upper Canada the rebellions were over, although the acrimony and bitterness would not fade away. Tories were outraged that some Reformers in the London District, who had formed political unions, had thought more of protecting themselves than of

Monument to Lount and Matthews in the Necropolis Cemetery, Toronto. The monument was not erected for some time after the executions of the men at the Toronto jail.

protecting the government. What followed the two brief risings was somehow a typical Canadian response — an over-reaction with mass arrests in the time of panic. When the excitement subsided few people were actually charged, and still fewer were punished. In Upper Canada no one was executed in the London District for taking part in the rebellion there, although Duncombe and Eliakim Malcolm might have paid with their lives, as would Mackenzie, had any of them been caught.

Yet for all the sense of outrage the majority of the populace felt, only two rebels, both from the Home District, were hanged, a fate which Anthony Van Egmond probably escaped by dying in jail in Toronto. Peter Matthews and Samuel Lount, however, went to the scaffold after their trials in April 1838. By attacking the capital they had aroused strong emotions among government supporters, and in a sense they were the scapegoats. They had to be made to pay, even though thousands favoured leniency towards them.

There were to be other executions, but in all cases the men who lost their lives had come into Upper Canada, whether American sympathizer or Canadian exile, to make trouble, and in nearly every instance loyal Canadians were killed. These incursions were much more alarming and violent than the original rebellions.

Chapter 6
The *Caroline*: an International Incident

While Colonel Allan MacNab was in the London District, the militia on the Niagara frontier remained on the alert. Parts of all five of the Lincoln militia regiments were embodied, but the most active officers appeared to be Colonel James Kerby of the 2nd Lincolns and Colonel Kenneth Cameron of the 5th. Cameron was the more experienced of the two, for he was a half-pay officer of the 79th Regiment. Kerby's men were drawn from Stamford, Thorold and Pelham townships, those in Cameron's from Grantham and Louth. Kerby's headquarters moved from Drummondville to Fort Erie, while Cameron's were at the town of Niagara (now Niagara-on-the-Lake). Sensitive spots were Queenston, the landing below the Falls, and Waterloo Ferry, above the Falls between Fort Erie and Chippawa. At first the militia had attempted to stop fleeing rebels, but after 11 December, when Mackenzie reached Buffalo, the excitement he roused in that city was cause for further alarm.

Buffalo was fertile ground for the seeds of Mackenzie's propaganda. The city of 25,000 had many labourers, and sailors from the Erie Canal, who were unemployed during the winter months. Unemployment, especially among the young men, was unusually high owing to the economic recession of 1837. Such were easily seduced by the little rebel's speeches that matched his fiery wig, and his promise of adventure and free land grants to all who would join an army of liberation. Colonel Kerby stationed some of his regiment and some of Colonel Samuel Street's 3rd Lincolns at Waterloo Ferry. The militiamen were accommodated in houses and barns; bedding, blankets and provisions were scarce. [1]

Mackenzie was befriended by Rensselaer Van Rensselaer, of Albany, a member of one of New York's fine old Dutch families, but an incompetent, hard-drinking adventurer. Together the journalist-politician exile and the decadent aristocrat hatched the plan for an army. They began referring to their followers, American sympathizers and Canadian refugees alike, as "Patriots", a decidedly inappropriate title. A more accurate name is "republicans" since their aim was severing the British connection and disposing of the monarchy.

William Kingsmill, commander of the incorporated militia battalion named the Queen's Own Regiment of Militia. Kingsmill was a half-pay captain who settled in Upper Canada after the Napoleonic Wars.

Mackenzie and Van Rensselaer resolved to occupy Navy Island, in Canadian waters, as their base of operation against the province. On the island, upstream from Chippawa, had been a shipyard during the French period, and its name was a translation of Ile de la Marine. On Wednesday 13 December, Mackenzie and Van Rensselaer rode in a scow with a party of some two dozen men (many of them Upper Canadians), to Grand Island, belonging to the United States, and on to Navy Island, arriving early on the morning of the 14th. There Mackenzie proclaimed his provisional government.

When Sir Francis Head learned that Mackenzie was in Buffalo, he wanted an Assistant Adjutant-General of Militia for the Niagara frontier, and he appointed Colonel Kenneth Cameron. Then when Head discovered that Mackenzie and Van Rensselaer were on Navy Island, he ordered Cameron to move his headquarters to Chippawa, from which village the tip of the island was visible. On the 18th, Head himself arrived by steamer at Niagara. That same day he appointed Richard Bullock, a half-pay officer from the 41st Regiment and high sheriff of the Midland District, Adjutant- General of Militia to succeed Colonel Coffin. Head reached Chippawa on the 19th, where he conferred with Colonel Cameron, and Colonel Kerby who rode over from Fort Erie. Head agreed that the militia detachments should be relieved at regular intervals, so that this duty would not put too much hardship on any one unit. [2]

Head sent a message to Hamilton for Colonel MacNab, ordering him to bring 300 volunteers and take command of operations on the Niagara frontier as soon as he returned from the London District. Back home on Christmas Eve, MacNab sent couriers to Oakville and other points, asking for the volunteers. Men not coming were to give any of the Queen's arms in their possession to those who volunteered. He told Colonel William Chisholm of the 2nd Gore Regiment to pay twenty shillings a day currency for each team of horses he needed to hire, to carry men and supplies from Oakville. Chisholm assembled a full company at Wellington Square (now part of Burlington) and followed after MacNab. [3]

The number of volunteers MacNab assembled was closer to 600, and included Captain John Poore and his company of Guelph Rifles. Writing to Judge Jonas Jones on Christmas Eve, MacNab reported that militia from Dundas and Paris had arrived in sleighs, and he would leave "tomorrow" taking a field piece. The ladies of Hamilton were making haversacks, and each man would bring a blanket and other necessaries. He had no news about stores on the Niagara frontier, but he hoped some were on the way. He had written to Colonel Kenneth Cameron that he was bringing seventy to eighty

Navy Island and the village of Chippawa, looking towards Niagara Falls. The rebels had a strong position on the island, and the militiamen were exposed to their fire.

dragoons, and he would need billets for his entire force. Proudly, MacNab informed Jones that he had not lost a man in the London District, although three were ill. [4]

More volunteers were on the way. From the Grand River, William Johnson Kerr brought Six Nations warriors eager to demonstrate their affection for the Crown. Samuel Peters Jarvis led 300 men from Toronto, including Captain Peregrine Warren's company of Cobourg Rifles and John Elmsley, an experienced Lake Ontario captain. Both were professionals, Warren a former captain of the 66th Regiment, Elmsley a lieutenant in the Royal Navy. James Sears formed a company of fifty Blacks at St. Catharines and set out for Chippawa. The Blacks were alarmed that the Americans, who enslaved their brethren, were aiding Mackenzie. [5] Other capable seamen joined the expedition. Andrew Drew, a half-pay officer in the Royal Navy who farmed near Woodstock, had accompanied MacNab from the London District. With William Chisholm went Edward Zealand, who had captained several steamboats, and Robert Wilson, the master of the schooner *Lady Colborne*. MacNab's force at Chippawa soon amounted to some 2,500 volunteers. Although the crisis of the rebellions was over, the province had not returned to normal and, in addition, large numbers of its citizens were suspected of harbouring pro-rebel sympathies. Thus, it was still easier to depend on volunteers rather than on the usual militia regiments, some of which were not properly organized and some of which contained men of questionable loyalty. Although parts of MacNab's force were drawn from existing regiments, it was also on a volunteer basis.

The supply situation was critical; bedding and food were even more scarce and, as in the London District, hasty arrangements had to be made. Although MacNab's men had travelled in sleighs, the weather was mild for the time of year. Farmers brought in wagon loads of beef and other commodities to sell for the use of the troops, and again record keeping was slipshod. Claims would go unsettled for

months or years. Because of his boundless confidence in MacNab, once the colonel was on the scene the lieutenant governor returned to Toronto.

Meanwhile, on Navy Island, Mackenzie and Van Rensselaer received more men and supplies, transported on a variety of vessels from Buffalo, and at least one cannon. The republicans erected fortifications and commenced firing on the militiamen drawn up along the shore to the east of Chippawa. To the exasperation of the volunteers, Head forbade MacNab taking anything but defensive action out of concern about a possible war with the United States. Some of the Lincoln Militia, miserable because of inadequate shelter and bedding, resorted to drink to combat the cold.

Confusing reports poured in regarding events on Navy Island. Spies from both sides were active, loyal ones bringing exaggerated

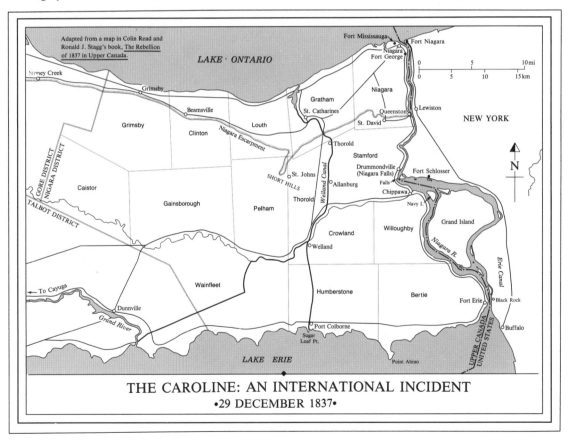

THE CAROLINE: AN INTERNATIONAL INCIDENT
•29 DECEMBER 1837•

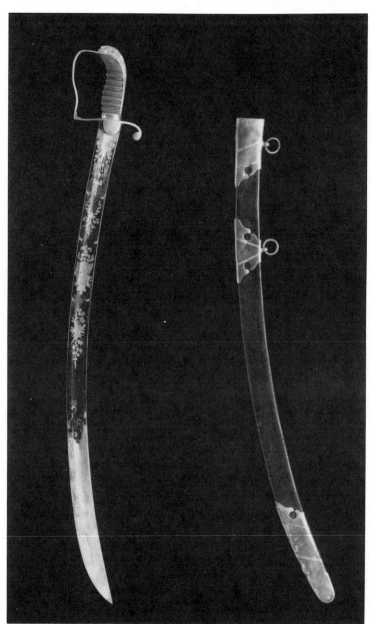

Andrew Drew in the uniform of an admiral 1846. The artist, H. Holmes, painted as the backdrop Niagara Falls and the wrecked *Caroline*.

Sword carried by Captain Andrew Drew while participating in the destruction of the American steamer *Caroline*. Legend maintains that Drew sported a cutlass.

intelligence on the strength of Mackenzie and Van Rensselaer's force. One who carried dispatches for the republicans, apparently, was a woman, Eunice Whiting, who was in Kingston Penitentiary three years later for stealing a horse.[6] On Christmas Eve, Alexander McLeod, a deputy sheriff for the Niagara District, returned to Chippawa from Buffalo and reported that some American enthusiasts planned to have the 26-ton steamer *Caroline* cut from the ice where she had been laid up for the winter. They intended to put her in service between Fort Schlosser (Niagara Falls, New York) and Navy Island.

On 28 December, MacNab and others observed the *Caroline* moving from the American side, supplying the republican force on the island. She also carried passengers, many of them only going for a visit to satisfy their curiosity. MacNab had appointed Andrew Drew the captain and commander of his naval force, and he sent him with McLeod to investigate. Drew and McLeod set off in a skiff and found the *Caroline* tied to a makeshift wharf on Navy Island. Some republicans noticed them and fired their rifles. The skiff was hit several times before the pair pulled out of range and returned safely to the Canadian side.

On the 29th, MacNab and Drew watched in frustration as the steamer plied back and forth, and they resolved to put a stop to the assistance she was giving the republicans. MacNab's decision was spurred by the increased firing from the island, which was making his militia ever more restive. He placed Drew in command of fifty eager volunteers. Most were experienced seamen, but MacNab allowed Captain Peregrine Warren, and his lieutenant, Sheppard McCormick, to join the expedition with a few of their Cobourg riflemen. Also present were Edward Zealand, John Elmsley and William Chisholm, but not Deputy Sheriff Alexander McLeod. (In 1840, McLeod was arrested in Lewiston, New York, after boasting of his part in the attack, and charged with murder and arson. Britain

Pen and ink drawing of the *Caroline* by William J. Thomson 1893, based on descriptions of the steamer.

BY
JOHN CHARLES DENT
AUTHOR OF "THE LAST FORTY YEARS" &C.

VOL. II.

The Cutting-out of the Caroline

TORONTO.
PUBLISHED BY C. BLACKETT ROBINSON
1885

Cutting out of the *Caroline,* by volunteers led by Captain Andrew Drew,
originally published in 1885.

demanded that McLeod be released, but American public opinion was so aroused that William Seward, then the governor of New York State, insisted on a trial. McLeod was acquitted of taking part in the destruction of the steamer because he had an ironclad alibi.) 7

Drew's men left the Canadian shore in oared boats at 9.00 p.m. on 29 December, many of the party armed with naval cutlasses, others with boarding pikes or firearms. They expected to find the *Caroline* at or close to Navy Island, in Canadian waters. They looked in vain for the steamer until they finally spotted her tied up at Fort Schlosser, in New York State. This nicely did not deter Captain Drew, nor any of other professionals with him. MacNab had ordered Drew to put the steamer out of action, and he went ahead.

The boats were within twenty yards of their quarry when a sentry challenged them. Drew responded by calling that he would give the countersign when he got aboard, which mollified the sentry, a man of scant military acumen. The boats moved in and the men threw up their boarding pikes. Witnesses reported that Drew was one of the first to reach the deck, cutlass between his teeth. In fact, he was carrying a sword. 8 He was soon well supported by the rest of his party. Aboard the *Caroline* they found ten crewmen and twenty-three others who could not find beds at an inn on shore. Drew's men roused them all and drove them to the wharf, but not without resistance and considerable noise.

In the scuffling Captain Warren and Lieutenant McCormick of the Cobourg Rifles, and one sailor named Reynolds were wounded.9 Drew sent Richard Arnold below to get up the steam so that they could take the steamer to Chippawa. Shouts were coming from a tavern on shore, and some of Drew's men dashed onto the wharf to untie the mooring lines, but they were driven back by republicans firing small arms. Arnold and some others found a tin containing oil, which they took to the ladies' cabin, poured it on some bedding and ignited it. Drew then ordered the *Caroline* towed into the river, to elude the republicans exiting from the tavern. Edward Zealand attempted to cut the lines, but he found that some were chains. John Elmsley led sixteen men to the wharf to cover the men near the tavern, to allow Zealand more time. Once the steamer was loose, the men got aboard their boats and followed the brightly burning *Caroline* out into the river.

The *Caroline* drifted towards the Falls, but did not, as the newspapers proclaimed, go over them. She grounded above the drop, but as she broke up many pieces, including her figurehead, did plunge over the Falls. The figurehead was rescued at Lewiston and was later placed in the museum of the Buffalo Historical Society. [10] The demise of the steamer caused a furor in New York State, and as word spread, all over the United States. Reports that many lives had been lost circulated. The governor of New York, William Marcy, claimed that a third of the people Drew found aboard the *Caroline* had been killed. Only one body was found, that of Amos Durfee of Buffalo, which lay in state at the City Hall. According to some versions Durfee was Black, [11] an irony in a country that allowed slavery.

Apart from any loss of life, the destruction of property was a serious matter, one that would haunt the British government for some time. The *Caroline* affair put a strain on Anglo-American relations even though Drew had not, technically, broken international law since the steamer had been contravening United States neutrality. The British government was embarrassed, and a controversy over whether MacNab had acted correctly would not

Propaganda picture of the destruction of the *Caroline*. Contrary to the impression given by the artist, W.R. Callington, an engineer, the steamer did not go over Niagara Falls. The picture appeared in a Fleet Street newspaper not long after the sinking on 29 December 1837.

Propaganda Report from the *Toronto Patriot* . The editorial appeared in the issue of Tuesday 2 January 1838.

die down. In the days that followed, the Canadian militiamen fired back more often against the gunners on Navy Island. Only one republican was reported killed, but three members of the militia lost their lives because the shore near Chippawa was an exposed position. [12]

News of the cutting out of the *Caroline* brought a rush of recruits to Navy Island. There, Mackenzie and Van Rensselaer were quarrelling. Van Rensselaer was drinking heavily, and neither man could decide what to do next with their "Patriot Army of the North-West". Dr. John Rolph went to the island but he only stayed an hour before leaving in disgust. Two devious characters said to have paid visits were Benjamin Lett and Bill Johnston.

Ben Lett was a native of Ireland whose family moved to Darlington Township, in Durham County, in 1833. He was an Orangeman, the exception to the rule that members of the lodge were loyal. Lett was suspected of doing a number of nasty deeds, but he was secretive. Bill Johnston was a man who could not keep quiet.

Johnston's parents were U.E. Loyalists, and he was born at Trois-Rivières in 1782. His family moved to the Bay of Quinte after the American Revolution. By most accounts it would appear Bill was virulently anti-British. But why so anti-British is a matter of debate. One tale suggested that he had been convicted of smuggling, another that he had refused to serve in the militia in the War of 1812 and crossed the border. He spied for the Americans during that war and later lived at French Creek (Clayton, New York). From various hideouts in the Thousand Islands, all called Fort Wallace, Bill led a band of men that travelled in a row galley and preyed on British shipping, which earned him the title "Pirate Bill". Van Rensselaer made him "Admiral of the Patriot Navy in the East", for which Bill was patently unsuited. He did not stay on Navy Island, if he went there, for he disliked long odds. Van Rensselaer had only 450 men to MacNab's 2,500. [13]

Back in Toronto, the Adjutant-General of Militia, Richard Bullock, was planning a more efficient force, with the approval of a still badly shaken Sir Francis Head. By a Militia General Order on 23 December, Bullock authorized two companies, each of sixty men, as a (Toronto) City Guard,[14] and, on 15 December he created the first two of six regiments of incorporated militia for permanent duty over the next six months, to 1 July 1838. The pay for the rank and file was to be eight dollars a month with free rations, and each men would be issued with a coat, trousers, shoes, stockings, mittens and a shirt. The families of the married men were to receive free rations, although this last was later rescinded. Each regiment, commanded by a full colonel, would have ten companies of fifty rank and file, and with the officers would amount to some 550 all ranks:

Regimental Name	Colonel-Commandant	Headquarters
Queen's Rangers	Samuel Peters Jarvis	Toronto
Queen's Light Infantry	Joseph Hill	Toronto
Royal Foresters	Arthur Carthew	Toronto
Queen's Own Regiment of Militia	William Kingsmill	Toronto
Queen's Niagara Fencibles	James Kerby	Fort Erie
Frontier Light Infantry	Kenneth Cameron	Niagara

The regiments, which were set up through December and January, were drawn from various locations. The Queen's Rangers and Queen's Light Infantry were raised in the Toronto area, while the Royal Foresters were chiefly Orangemen from Simcoe County. Where possible the regiments were created out of existing ones. On 24 January, the 1st and 2nd regiments became the Queen's Niagara Fencibles and the 1st Frontier Light Infantry.[15]

Kingsmill's Queen's Own was drawn from Durham, Northumberland, and Prince Edward Counties. It was created out of a group of 700 volunteers which Bullock ordered raised, on 30 December. Each recruit was to provide himself with a serviceable firelock and thirty rounds of ball cartridge or other ammunition, for which he would be compensated. The other terms of enlistment were the same as for the other regiments. The volunteers would be drawn from regiments located at or near:

Durham County	125
Northumberland	125
Prince Edward	150
Town of Kingston	100
Town of Perth and vicinity	100
Simcoe County	100 [16]

A third company was added to the Toronto City Guard, and Mayor George Gurnett was appointed the commander, with the rank of major. Bullock also authorized Captain Thomas Runchey of St.

Catharines to raise a new Black corps of seventy-seven privates for four months service.

The republicans on Navy Island hoped to land on Canadian soil, but their attempts to obtain a steamer were foiled. They tried to acquire the *Barcelona* but they were outbid by General Winfield Scott of the United States Army, who took over the steamer. Scott had been dispatched to the frontier by President Van Buren to prevent violations of the Neutrality Act by American citizens. Help was on the way for Upper Canada as well. Sir John Colborne received reinforcements of regular troops from New Brunswick and Nova Scotia, and he dispatched the 24th Regiment at the end of December. Lieutenant-Colonel Charles Hughes and the vanguard of his men reached Kingston by the 30th. They were met by Colonel Colley Foster, who had gone to Kingston to oversee the movement of supplies for Toronto. Lieutenant Frederick Chetwood and half a company of the 24th were posted to Carillon, on the Ottawa River, to guard the Grenville Canal. [17]

Colonel Allan MacNab was superseded, but he did not surrender his command gracefully. When Lieutenant-Colonel Hughes arrived at Chippawa on 11 January, MacNab objected to the arrangement whereby a regular officer of lower rank would replace him and leave the command of the 24th Regiment to Major Henry Dive Townshend. Numbers, MacNab asserted in a letter to Head, were on the side of the militia, which had 305 officers and 3,262 other ranks on the Niagara frontier. The 24th had only 18 officers and 375 other ranks. MacNab informed Head that he would not "play second fiddle" and he preferred to depart rather than accept a subordinate role. [18]

Colonel Foster soon arrived, and he set up headquarters at Niagara, while Hughes made his at Drummondville. Neither officer approved of MacNab's handling of the *Caroline* affair. He had behaved like the rank amateur he was, and Andrew Drew's part was even more reprehensible. He was a professional naval officer, who should have seen the implications of destroying a ship belonging to a foreign power in peacetime, and within that power's boundaries.

The republicans on Navy Island decided, since they had no hope of a successful invasion, to evacuate their position. They started moving to Grand Island on 13 January, and the following day they began arriving in Buffalo. The Upper Canadian Militia occupied the island on the 15th, and Sir Francis Head came to inspect the encampment on the 17th. A disgusting mess confronted the lieutenant governor — wretched huts, leftover food, refuse and assorted filthy clothing.

MacNab returned to Dundurn Castle, Head to Government House. Later MacNab was knighted for his services in the Home and London Districts, but not for vanquishing the *Caroline*. Lieutenant-Colonel Hughes remained in command of the Niagara frontier. Colonel Foster moved his headquarters back to Toronto, where Captain John Simcoe Macaulay of the Royal Engineers had assumed command of the militia garrison, with the local rank of colonel. Macaulay was the son of an army surgeon who had served with John Graves Simcoe during the American Revolution.

In Washington, President Van Buren issued a proclamation that Americans who took part in armed invasions would not he protected if they were caught. [19] More regulars were on their way from Lower Canada. The volunteers would continue to have a vital role, but they would no longer be unsupported. In Toronto the Adjutant General's office began the long slow process of building up the decayed militia structure. The *Upper Canada Gazette*, which carried government notices, was filled with militia general orders appointing officers and creating new sedentary regiments. Each time there was a strong threat of invasion over the next year, the process would be repeated. At times when the threat was not as great, far fewer appointments were made.

PART II
STANDING ARMY

The continued disturbances of the American-Canadian frontier after the rebellions forced military authorities in both provinces to mobilize the first standing Canadian army in peacetime.

Elinor Kyte Senior, *From Royal Township to Industrial City: Cornwall 1784-1984* (Belleville 1983), p. 146.

Chapter 7

Alarms, January and February 1838

M ackenzie was still on Navy Island when Canadian exiles and American sympathizers became active in Detroit. There the "Patriot Army of the North West" (a shadowy organization of Canadian rebels and American sympathizers) had stolen 400 "rifles" from the jail. On 8 January, Stevens Thomson Mason, the governor of Michigan, ordered the republicans to disband or leave the United States. In response, what purported to be 700 republicans set out in a small fleet from Gibraltar, a village some twenty miles below Detroit, for Bois Blanc Island, close to Amherstburg. Their leader was Irish-born Edward Theller, who assumed the imposing title of "Brigadier-General to command the first Brigade of French and Irish troops to be raised in Canada." The actual number of Theller's force was closer to 200. [1]

The three regiments of Essex County Militia were more neglected than those in most of the other districts. Nevertheless, Lieutenant-Colonel (later Colonel) John Prince of the 3rd Essex, drawn from Colchester, Gosfield and Mersea Townships, had embodied some men and posted them along the Detroit River.

John Prince had practised law in Cheltenham, England, before moving to Upper Canada in 1833. He established Park Farm, on the fringe of Sandwich village, and he was soon appointed a magistrate. He had brought substantial funds to establish himself in the colonies, and was a member of the legislature. Although coming from a genteel town like Cheltenham, Prince was a wild man, unpredictable and prone to violent behaviour. He kept a diary in which he

recorded horsewhipping Charles Baby, a son of the Honourable James Baby, because he did not like Charles' reply to a challenge to a duel. The most active militia commander on the Detroit frontier, Prince went to see Governor Mason on 18 December 1837 to inform

Capture of Navy Island by government supporters. In truth the rebels abandoned the island before any government forces arrived. The cartoon appeared in an American account of the rebellions.

The Reverend Josiah Henson, who served in Amherstburg after the rebellions. Blacks were among the most reliable troops for service on the frontiers because they viewed Americans as implacable enemies for tolerating slavery.

him that the discontent in Upper Canada was greatly exaggerated. [2]

Among the volunteers who were serving with Prince was a small company of Black men commanded by the Reverend Josiah Henson, who was then living at Windsor village, above Sandwich. Henson, best known as the man who inspired Harriet Beecher Stowe to write Uncle Tom's Cabin, had taken his men to defend Fort Malden at Amherstburg that December. As well, Colonel Thomas Radcliffe of the 2nd Middlesex Regiment, a half-pay officer from the 27th Regiment, brought a strong detachment from Adelaide Township in the London District. These volunteers later called themselves the Western Rangers. [3]

On learning that the enemy fleet had left Gibraltar, Prince moved 300 militia infantry and cavalry by steamer to Bois Blanc Island, but the republicans put in at Sugar Island, in American waters. Towards evening on the 8th, the militia on Bois Blanc noticed a boat making for their shore, and, since the town was vulnerable, they returned to Amherstburg. One of the republican vessels, the schooner Anne, sailed towards Fort Malden, above Amherstburg, and the vessel which had just arrived with Radcliffe and his men aboard, gave chase. The schooner fired a round of cannister shot at the militiamen positioned on Gordon's wharf, and turned towards Sugar Island. The militia returned the fire but did no damage.

The next day, 9 January, a party of republicans occupied the now deserted Bois Blanc Island, while Edward Theller, aboard the Anne, and others on a small sloop, the Geo. Strong, cruised in the vicinity, battering buildings on the Canadian shore. At 7.00 p.m. the Anne ran aground while attempting to sail to Bois Blanc Island. Anticipating a republican landing, the militia gathered close and began firing on the schooner. Some waded waist-deep in the icy water and, while a republican attempted to reload a cannon, captured the Anne. They found twenty-one men aboard, one of them dead and eight wounded. Among the wounded were Theller, who recovered, and David Anderson of Yarmouth, who had taken part in Duncombe's rising and who soon died. [4] Meanwhile the republicans on Bois Blanc Island, instead of joining the Anne in her attack, retreated to Sugar Island.

Militia from Kent County arrived, and Dr. William Dunlop embodied some men in the Huron Tract. Lieutenant-Colonel Joseph Brant Clench of the 5th Middlesex Regiment, who was part Mohawk, brought 200 Delaware Indians. Major John B. Askin and others in the London District had formed the London Volunteers and were forwarding supplies.[5] Thomas Radcliffe reported finding aboard the Anne enough muskets and bayonets to equip from 200 to 300 men, three field guns and some ammunition as well as $600 in cash. Theller expected to arm supporters he thought would be waiting for him.[6] Instead, he found himself bound for prison.

In Toronto, Adjutant-General of Militia Bullock authorized the formation of more independent companies for permanent duty, (including two small volunteer companies to serve at Sandwich and Amherstburg), especially cavalry for dispatch carrying and keeping lines of communication open. Sir Francis Head was busy arranging for the expenses incurred by the militia to be paid. Although Colonel

Foster had signed the accounts, Head reported that the provincial treasurer (in fact the receiver general, John Henry Dunn) had refused them on the grounds that the records had not been kept properly.

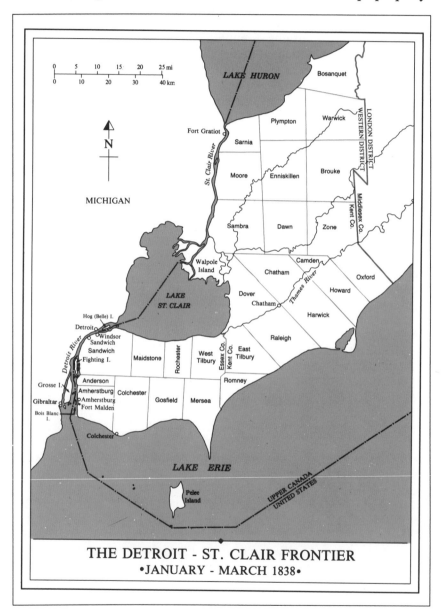

THE DETROIT - ST. CLAIR FRONTIER
•JANUARY - MARCH 1838•

Head appointed a board under the inspector general, George Herkimer Markland, to investigate the expenses. [7]

The incident over Bois Blanc Island, while minor, was a foretaste of disturbances emanating from border states that would cause the British government to keep a standing army in both the Canadas for more than three years. The 24th Regiment was only the vanguard. Ultimately the equivalent of nine battalions of regular troops would occupy Upper Canada. Unlike the militia, regulars were clothed in colourful uniforms, although in winter much of the uniform was concealed under a grey greatcoat. Beneath the greatcoat the swallow-tailed scarlet coatee of the 24th was faced green, and the dark grey trousers had a red welt down each side. The tall, bell-shaped shako (referred to as a cap) was designed to give a soldier extra height. The coatees of the rank and file had pewter buttons; the officers' buttons, lace and some accoutrements were gilded. The colour party carried two flags of lustrous, thick silk. One was the Union Jack and referred to as the Queen's Colour. The other, known as the Second or Regimental Colour, matched the facings on the uniforms, and had a Union Jack in the upper quarter adjoining the staff. Embroidered on the centre of each flag were the regimental number and devices. [8] The 24th was shabby after having been on duty in Upper Canada and in action against the rebels in the lower province.

In mid-January a second regiment, the 32nd (Cornwall), was on the way from Montreal under the command of Lieutenant-Colonel the Honourable John Maitland. The first five companies reached Kingston on the 14th. The sixth soon followed, with two companies of the 83rd Regiment. Unlike the 24th and 32nd, the 83rd had no regional name, although it became the County of Dublin Regiment of Foot in 1859. The 83rd was being moved in stages from New Brunswick to Upper Canada. The first five companies of the 32nd had an easy passage, by steamer from Prescott to Toronto. The rest had to go ashore below Gananoque and march to Kingston because the St. Lawrence had begun to freeze over. The men of the 32nd and 83rd travelled in sleighs on to London, where Maitland established his headquarters.

Until 1825 a British infantry regiment consisted of ten companies. That year the British army was reorganized so that only part of each regiment was used for active duty. Under the new regulations a regiment was still comprised of ten companies, but only six were active. These companies were known as service companies. The other four companies remained at the regimental

John Simcoe Macaulay, commander of the Toronto garrison following the risings on Yonge Street and in the London District. Macaulay's father, an army surgeon, had been a friend of Lieutenant Governor John Graves Simcoe.

shore, where both Head and Colborne had confidence in the ability of the militia regiments to cope with any border crossings. Except for small pockets of disaffection the people were loyal, and Kingston, under Major Bonnycastle's watchful eye, was secure. To ease overcrowding in London, Hamilton and Toronto, some prisoners were forwarded to Fort Henry, the strongest place in the

Captain (left) and private (right) of the 83rd Regiment of Foot 1838. This regular regiment garrisoned Kingston after serving in Lower Canada. Until June 1837 the regiment had been quartered in Halifax, Nova Scotia. Here and in the illustrations on pages 83, 92 and 127, British regulars are depicted wearing the uniform of 1838 except for the higher "Albert" shako introduced in the 1840s. Bell top shakos were worn at the time of the Rebellions.

headquarters in Britain and were known as depot companies. The lieutenant-colonel commanded the service (active) portion, and each of the six companies had eighty-six privates. The depot portion was commanded by a major, and each of the four companies had fifty-six privates. Replacements for the service portion were drawn from the depot portion. Men not fit for active service were sent home to the depot companies.[9]

The 24th Regiment continued serving on the Niagara frontier. The 32nd and the two companies of the 83rd that were stationed in London, with an advance post at Chatham, were in a position to cover the western frontier, as well as the restive populace in the London District. The other sensitive area was the St. Lawrence province. Parts of the 1st Glengarry Regiment under Colonel Alexander Fraser and the 2nd Glengarry under Colonel Donald Macdonell were ordered to Lower Canada on 1 February by Sir John Colborne to help in disarming the disaffected there.[10] Colonel Macdonell is identified as belonging to the Greenfield branch of the family, to distinguish him from Colonel Donald Aeneas Macdonell of the 1st Stormont Regiment and other Donald Macdonells who held high rank in the Glengarry Militia. (People in Glengarry County still claim that the kilted Highlanders who went to Lower Canada appropriated so many horses that they left home as infantry and returned as cavalry.) By the time the Glengarries were on the march, many of the other men embodied from the sedentary militia of Upper Canada were being allowed to go home.

When the 32nd Regiment moved to Upper Canada, Sir John Colborne began formulating a new policy for the deployment of regular soldiers, one he would continue throughout the border troubles, with certain exceptions. To an underpaid, brutally disciplined regular, the United States seemed a land of promise. The temptation to desert from border stations was so great that Colborne did not want regular troops at such posts unless absolutely necessary. Thus most of the 24th was kept at Drummondville, close to Niagara Falls and away from easy crossing points at Queenston and Waterloo Ferry. From London and Chatham, safely inland, Lieutenant-Colonel Maitland could keep troops for counter attacks if any republicans crossed the Detroit River. The militia would be used to patrol the frontiers.

Among the most reliable for border work were the Black companies, whose members had no incentive to desert to the United States, and the cavalry. Dragoons had to provide their own horses and thus had a stake in ensuring that their mounts were not stolen or injured. [11]

As February progressed, enlistments in the regiments of incorporated militia were increasing, although none were at full strength. On 20 January, Colonel James Kerby's Queen's Niagara Fencibles had 417 men organized under nine captains. Colonel Kenneth Cameron's Frontier Light Infantry was somewhat larger. [12] As an added precaution, Colonel Foster arranged for Colonel Joseph Hill to move his Queen's Light Infantry from Toronto to Niagara, where Hill made his headquarters in tumble-down Fort George. [13] A return of the Toronto garrison for 5 February 1838 showed the strength of the other three incorporated regiments and miscellaneous smaller units:

Name of Unit	Officers	N.C.Os	Privates	Horses
Queen's Lancers (Magrath's)	3	6	47	58
Queen's Light Dragoons	3	7	47	59
1st Provincial Artillery	6	8	28	
Queen's Rangers (Jarvis')	33	65	406	
Royal Foresters (Carthew's)	33	51	358	
Queen's Own (Kingsmill's)	29	33	472	
Durham Volunteers	3	8	67	
City Guard (Gurnett's)	11	20	172	
Bank Guard	3	4	27[14]	
Total	124	202	1,624	117

By the middle of the month Kerby had 35 officers and 535 rank and file; Cameron had 48 officers and 671 rank and file. Sir John Colborne authorized uniforms similar to those worn by the regulars — scarlet coatees faced blue and grey trousers. All militia officers would have silver lace and accoutrements, and for undress, long blue frock coats similar to those permitted regular officers.[15] However, the uniforms were slow to materialize.

In all the sensitive areas the gathering of intelligence and disposing of spies were of vital importance. From Fort Erie, Colonel Kerby had his agents working around Buffalo, and he was in communication with the United States army and naval officers about republican activities. President Van Buren had dispatched General Winfield Scott and allowed him a few troops, but the American regular army was small and heavily committed to fighting the Indians along the frontiers. The small detachments of American soldiers stationed near Sackets Harbor, Buffalo and Detroit were

Richard Bonnycastle, major in the Royal Engineers and colonel in the militia. Bonnycastle was knighted for his services for the defence of Kingston in 1837.

almost powerless against determined republicans bent on crossing into Upper Canada.

At Kingston, Major Bonnycastle had his sources of information and was aware that Americans were coming into the town to observe military preparations and to recruit for the republican cause. He caught a justice of the peace from Watertown, New York, "boasting in the streets of Kingston, to an admiring multitude, that we ought to be dreadfully frightened at the preparation of our friendly adversaries." The man was accompanied by an American militia officer. Before they left, Bonnycastle marched a body of militia, uniformed and well-drilled, under the window of the inn where the Americans were staying and had the soldiers practice street firing. A friend of Bonnycastle's engaged the officer in conversation.

On being asked whether those were British infantry, the friend replied, "Oh no, not at all, they are only the Frontenac Militia."

"Then if they are Militia," retorts the American officer, "all I can say is, they must be *Regular* Militia." [16]

After leaving Navy Island, Mackenzie went on a speaking tour to Rochester and through the counties of New York State that bordered to St. Lawrence River, seeking to provoke a declaration of war on Britain. Bonnycastle heard rumours of an intended attack on Kingston, and he was on the alert for "reconnoitering parties" sent by Van Rensselaer, who was reported to be raising an army for Mackenzie. January had been unusually mild, allowing steamboats to operate longer than usual. February turned bitterly cold, the ice on the St. Lawrence was thick enough to support the weight of heavily laden sleighs, and Kingston was more vulnerable. Bonnycastle's sources warned him that the attack would come from three directions — from Belleville by road, Watertown over the ice, and across the ice from Clayton on the south shore of the St. Lawrence. The republicans who gathered at Clayton would go to American-owned Grindstone Island, and on to tiny Hickory Island, in Canadian waters. Mackenzie would accompany Van Rensselaer, who expected to make a feint towards Gananoque. That would draw militia to defend the mills in Gananoque while republicans from Belleville and Watertown moved directly towards Kingston.

The expected date of the attack was 22 February. As rumours spread, some Kingston residents brought Bonnycastle their valuables to be locked in Fort Henry. Acting on the rumours, Bonnycastle fitted up blockhouses that commanded the entrances to the town, and placed militia in barracks between them. He alerted the militia officers in Prince Edward County to assemble near Napanee, where dissidents were thought to be numerous, and asked that men be sent to Belleville to watch the disaffected there. One of his adjutants, Captain Angus Cameron, took a party to cut irregular holes in the ice near Wolfe Island, to entrap sleighs. Cameron's men also blocked the main road by felling trees. Mohawk warriors from Tyendinaga on the Bay of Quinte arrived, and Bonnycastle sent them out to patrol, disguised as deer hunting parties. On discovering that one of Bill Johnston's men had enlisted in the militia in order to spike the guns at Fort Henry, Bonnycastle dismissed him and ordered him out of the country, warning him to expect no mercy if he returned.

On the evening of 21 February, Bonnycastle learned that the Prince Edward Militia was stopping rebels who had marched near

Napanee and had taken some prisoners. Bonnycastle put guards on inns where sympathisers might be lodging, and mustered the 1st Frontenac Regiment, then in the Tete de Pont barracks. Lieutenant-Colonel Cubitt was ill, but he barricaded himself and his company of artillerymen, with some militia, inside Fort Henry and prepared to defend it. Kingston's town major, Thomas Fitzgerald, set out with a company of loyal Belleville riflemen and a party of Indians for Gananoque.

The village was already preparing. Elizabeth Barnett, a school teacher with friends in Clayton, had returned over the ice from a visit and warned the officers of the 2nd Leeds Regiment that republicans expected to gather on Grindstone Island shortly. By 21 February scarcely 300 men had reached Hickory Island. Mackenzie and Van Rensselaer, with Bill Johnston in tow, decided to abandon the venture because of the poor turnout. They started back to Grindstone Island, and not a moment too soon. Militiamen had begun to

advance across the ice from Gananoque. The volunteers captured some stragglers, whom they escorted to Fort Henry. [17]

Bonnycastle was delighted with the zeal the militia demonstrated, even though it sometimes got out of hand. One sentry, posted to the bridge over the Cataraqui River, ordered the four-horse mail sleigh from Montreal to halt. The driver ignored him, and the sentry stopped the sleigh by plunging his bayonet into the chest of a lead horse. Someone complained to the postmaster general, but Bonnycastle promoted the militiaman. A return for 1 March showed that the force at Kingston was composed of some 1,300 men embodied from the sedentary militia of the counties of Frontenac, Lennox and Addington, Prince Edward, Hastings and Lanark, and nearly 500 volunteers, as well as three chiefs and 70 Mohawk warriors from the Bay of Quinte. Most were concentrated in the town, but detachments were deployed at Napanee, Gananoque and the Kingston Mills locks on the Rideau Canal. Dragoons posted

Home of Richard Bonnycastle in Toronto. The Bonnycastle house stood on the south side of Front Street West, opposite Peter Street. It had been occupied by Colonel Nathaniel Coffin when he was adjutant-general of militia.

every few miles were keeping communications open, and twelve other Mohawks were serving as scouts. [18]

The attempt to capture Kingston ended in a farce, but 25 February brought two more scares, one at Niagara, the other at Sandwich on the Detroit River. At Fort Erie, Colonel Kerby received word from Colonel William Worth of the United States Army, who was stationed in Buffalo, that men were assembling arms at Comstock's Tavern, eight miles away near the Lake Erie shore. Kerby sent two militia companies west to Point Abino, while Worth pursued the republicans in a revenue cutter and turned them back. [19]

The occupation of Fighting Island, below Sandwich, was almost a comic opera. The republicans were led, more or less, by Dr. Charles Duncombe and another Canadian exile, "General" Donald McLeod, an ex-British Army sergeant, who had been a teacher in Belleville and Prescott, a journalist, and a major in the Grenville militia. [20] The Detroit town guard had been trying to curb the republicans, but on 23 February the steamer *Erie* slipped away with some of them aboard. When the town guard moved in, the republicans left a wagon full of ammunition on the dock, which was quickly hauled off to a rendez-vous — the Rising Sun Tavern outside the town. From that vicinity the *Erie* carried some republicans, their ammunition and weapons, to Fighting Island. The next day, the 24th, more republicans gathered on the shore opposite the island, and were joined by Donald McLeod, who had led a party of men from Cleveland during the night. All told, about 150 republicans reached Fighting Island, but they had only 50 muskets and a 6-pounder cannon "borrowed" from the arsenal at Dearborn, Michigan. McLeod waited for more supplies before advancing.

General Hugh Brady of the United States Army sent a message to Sandwich, which Colonel John Prince relayed to Lieutenant-Colonel Maitland who had recently arrived at Fort Malden with three companies of his 32nd Regiment, two of the 24th, and two of the 83rd, to reinforce Major H. D. Townshend of the 24th. Townshend had been at the fort since the end of January with one company of the 24th and two of the 32nd. Maitland sent Townshend to deal with the invaders. After reconnoitering on the evening of the 24th with the St. Thomas Volunteer Cavalry, the Major was joined the next morning by two companies from Malden, a detachment of the Royal Artillery with one field piece and 300 to 400 militia. The cannon fired a number of rounds into the invaders wounding several men, and causing new panic among the republicans. Then, finding a path across the ice, Townshend ordered his men to advance in single file,

regulars first. Colonel Prince, at the time serving as a volunteer rather than a ranking officer, had some militiamen put planks over a hole in the ice. Townshend placed his regulars on either side of the small island, facing the American shore, while he led the centre, flanked by volunteers. At the sight of the advancing troops the republicans began to flee over the ice. Five were wounded, but only one was captured, while Maitland had no casualties. When the republicans reached the American side they were dispersed by United States regulars.

A much more serious encounter began on 26 February. The ice was thick in places, and 400 republicans left Sandusky, Ohio, in sleighs and effected a landing on Pelee Island, to the south of Point Pelee in Lake Erie. Command of this vanguard was in the hands of "Colonels" H.C. Seward and E.D. Bradley, "Major" Lester Hoadley and "Captain" George Van Rensselaer (a relative of Mackenzie's hapless "General"). Their superior officer, "Brigadier-General" Thomas Jefferson Sutherland, was not yet on the scene. His followers were almost entirely Americans, who saw themselves as liberators amd assumed that the Upper Canadians had caught the "Spirit of '76". The "liberators" began by making prisoners of the few inhabitants they encountered, chiefly the family of William McCormick, the principal land holder. McCormick himself escaped and set out for Amherstburg. The republicans meanwhile made the large stone McCormick house their headquarters.

McCormick reached Amherstburg, bringing the first news of the republican's presence on Canadian soil. Lieutenant-Colonel Maitland sent Captain George Glasgow, of the Royal Artillery, to determine whether the ice was strong enough to support artillery. Glasgow returned at noon on 2 March (a Friday) and reported that the ice was thick but covered with many snow drifts. Maitland requisitioned sleighs, and the procession left Amherstburg at 6.00 p.m. He took the four companies of his 32nd Regiment, one company of the 83rd, and a detachment of the Royal Artillery and two 6-pounders under Captain Glasgow, about 300 men all told. He prayed that the invading force was small, because the men of his own 32nd Regiment were young, for the most part green recruits who had never been under fire. His militia comprised twenty-one St. Thomas cavalrymen under Captain James Ermatinger, one company of mounted volunteers led by Lieutenant-Colonel John Prince and his major, Prideaux Girty of Gosfield Township, and some Indians. Maitland's pilot was Captain W. Fox of the lst Essex Regiment. Fox had difficulty finding the poorly packed trail along the icebound shore of Lake Erie, and a cavalryman rode off in search of a lantern. Even with this light, the path was not easy to follow. Worse, the bobbing lantern alerted the republicans on Pelee Island, ruling out the advantage of surprise.

Maitland had hoped to attack at dawn on the 3rd, but his force did not reach the village of Colchester until 10.00 p.m. on the 2nd. After a pause to rest the horses, the punitive expedition continued at 2.00 a.m. Meanwhile, the republicans on Pelee freed their captives and withdrew from the northern part of the island into nearly impenetrable forest and bush that covered the southern part, a strong defensive position. Six more sleighs loaded with republicans had reached Pelee Island, but these departed carrying most of the reinforcements with them.

Maitland's expedition was within a mile of Pelee Island shortly after first light, and he resolved to entrap the republicans by cutting off their line of retreat. He sent Captain George Browne with the lst and 2nd companies of the 32nd Regiment, twenty-one St. Thomas and four Sandwich cavalrymen under Captain James Ermatinger, and six Indians, to the south of the island. Indian scouts soon informed Browne that republicans numbering 300 to 400 were approaching his position, and Captain Ermatinger, patrolling, sent a courier to Maitland asking for reinforcements and rode close to the regulars' position. Browne's infantry numbered ninety-five, the 2nd company of the 32nd commanded by Captain John Henry Evelegh. The regulars left their sleighs and formed close ranks, under orders to remain steady until ordered to fire. Upon hearing the order for an American advance, Browne, outnumbered perhaps three to one, placed his men three paces apart, to make his force seem larger.[21]

Meanwhile, Maitland's main body, with the two artillery pieces, reached the north shore of Pelee Island, where he intended routing the invaders by driving them southwards into the woods and towards Browne's force. He found a deserted encampment close to the shore, but pursuit was difficult because of the depth of the snow and the thickness of the woods.

Thus the main skirmish occurred, not with Maitland's centre, but with Captain Browne's covering force. American riflemen, perhaps forty, were the first to approach, followed by what appeared a strong line under "Captain" George Van Rensselaer. For some twenty minutes the firing was brisk on both sides, the regulars suffering many casualties. Worried that his losses might be horrendous, Browne ordered his men to fix bayonets and charge. The charge, accompanied by the shouts of the professionals, proved

View of Amherstburg from the south-southeast in 1821, by Major John Elliott Woolford. The scene would not have changed much by 1837.

Fort Malden, at Amherstburg, as it appeared in 1894.

the undoing of the republican force. They broke and fled and the battle was over. Browne's men took eleven prisoners, five of them badly wounded. British losses were four regulars and Thomas Parish of the St. Thomas cavalry killed, and some thirty regulars wounded. Exactly how many invaders died was not established; the information was contradictory. Hoadley and Van Rensselaer were killed, and some republicans drowned when they broke through the ice during their flight. Captain Ermatinger tried to lead the cavalry in pursuit, but he turned back when the ice gave way under his horse's hooves. [22]

Concerned for the welfare of his many wounded, Maitland ordered a return to Amherstburg with all possible speed. The regulars set out shortly, and were back at their base by 11.00 o'clock that same night. Colonel John Prince, Major Prideaux Girty and many of the militia lingered at Colchester until the morning of Sunday 4 March before following after Maitland's regulars and the prisoners captured in the battle. About seven miles from Amherstburg, Prince and Girty, riding in a sleigh, spotted two figures on the ice. Prince and another officer took two one-horse cutters and gave chase. As Prince drew near, he recognized "Brigadier" Sutherland and his aide-de-camp, "Captain" Patrick Spencer, walking across the ice from the American side. When Sutherland attempted to draw his sword, Prince ordered him to leave it where it was or he would shoot him. [23]

The month of March brought a change in the administration. Major-General Sir George Arthur arrived from Britain to succeed Sir Francis Bond Head, and he found the province in a highly emotional state. With the coming of Arthur the standing army would soon be better organized.

Courthouse and jail in 1829 when Toronto was still known as York. Prisoners were held and tried here in the spring of 1838, and Matthews and Lount were hanged outside the jail.

Chapter 8
Arthur Takes the Helm

As a career soldier, Sir George Arthur was well equipped to oversee the regulars and the militia. In administering a province racked by dissent and threatened from outside, he was determined not to do anything that might be construed as unconstitutional. Unlike Head, Arthur had experience. His previous appointment had been as the lieutenant governor of Van Diemen's Land (Tasmania), a settlement mainly of convicts. He was probably the right man in the right place. The burning question in Upper Canada in 1838 was not so much reform as survival. Arthur has been called despotic, but he had few options. Too much leniency towards captured insurgents would lose him the good will of the loyal majority on whom he had to depend in the event of further border disturbances. Regulars could provide the required steadiness, but never the numbers — as Colonel MacNab, now Sir Allan, had once pointed out to Sir Francis Head.

Arthur reached Toronto on 23 March, and Head left the next day. The former lieutenant governor intended making a quiet exit by steamer to Quebec City and Halifax and then by warship to England. Head was accompanied from Toronto by Judge Jonas Jones, but chose at the last minute to go through the United States, after several warnings, including one from Sir John Colborne, that he was to be murdered on his way to Halifax. The two embarked from Kingston in a small boat through blocks of ice for Cape Vincent, New York. Despite being recognized several times and at one point pursued by a group of horsemen whose purpose was unclear, Head and Jones reached New York City without serious trouble. Head was treated well by the Americans during the week he waited for the packet to take him home despite his fears of retaliation for the sinking of the *Caroline*. [1]

Arthur now faced the problems that menaced the province, from within and without. Upper Canada's economic life had been almost paralyzed. All public work had ceased, and agriculture was disrupted by the many alarms and militia duty. In some areas the situation resembled a civil war, as loyal people sought out those who might be in sympathy with the insurgents. Some militiamen seized

Sir George Arthur, lieutenant governor of Upper Canada from 1838 until 1840. Arthur succeeded Sir Francis Head in March 1838, and had to cope with the border raids.

the opportunity to settle old scores. Although the republicans across the border had been quiet since the drubbing they received at Pelee Island, rumours were rife that plotters were intending fresh incursions. Vigilance could not be relaxed.

The 24th Regiment moved to Toronto, leaving the defence of the Niagara frontier to three regiments of incorporated militia — Cameron's Frontier Light Infantry, Kerby's Queen's Niagara Fencibles, and Hill's Queen's Light Infantry — and detachments sent from the Toronto garrison. Colonel Kingsmill went to Point Abino with three companies of his Queen's Own. Colonel Kerby asked that some of Thomas Magrath's Queen's Lancers be sent to him for he was short of cavalry. Magrath, now a major, had been dispatched to London to assist Lieutenant-Colonel John Maitland.

A stream of people was leaving the province for the United States, because of fear of neighbours, or to look for land where their lives would not be disrupted. Reformers Peter Perry and Francis Hincks started a Mississippi Emigration Society. They failed to obtain a grant of land from the United States government, but individuals were pulling up stakes and selling their farms for a fraction of their value.[2] In this atmosphere of disillusionment and fear the trials of the rebels were taking place, in late March and early April.

The preliminary work had been done by boards of magistrates at London and Toronto, which Head had established in December, while individual magistrates questioned suspects in other areas. Many prisoners had been freed after examination, but some 300 to 400 were still in custody. The legislature passed a statute allowing prisoners to plead for mercy, for, as Chief Justice Robinson warned, trying so many people for treason would be very expensive. He hoped that just the ringleaders could be identified and tried.[3]

The executive council decided to make examples of Peter Matthews and Samuel Lount. Matthews had been captured first, by a party of militiamen who were led by an informer to the farmhouse of John Duncan in York Township. Lount almost succeeded in escaping. With Edward Kennedy he reached Lake Erie, but a storm blew their small boat to the mouth of the Grand River. They were captured by a farmer who took them for smugglers, and conveyed to Chippawa. There William Nelles of Grimsby, an officer in the 5th Lincolns, identified Lount.[4]

Matthews and Lount were tried before Chief Justice Robinson, pleaded guilty, and both were condemned to death. Despite petitions

Peter Matthews, who, with Samuel Lount, was hanged outside the Toronto jail for his part in the rebellions. His home was in Pickering Township, east of Toronto.

bearing thousands of signatures, and an appeal from Mrs. Lount on her knees before the lieutenant governor, the executive council remained adamant. The councillors maintained that any concession to the rebels would infuriate more people than it would appease. Arthur also felt that while the majority of rebels should be treated with leniency, a few examples had to be made from among the most guilty. The two family men — Lount had six children; Matthews had eight and two stepchildren — had to be sacrificed. Both were hanged in public outside the jail in Toronto on 12 April. Two days later Arthur wrote to the colonial secretary, Lord Glenelg, that there would not be any more executions. All other sentences could be commuted to transportation to a penal colony, a punishment with which he was all too familiar, or in most other cases, an absolute pardon could be given. [5]

Arthur now turned his attention to improving his military organization. He assumed direct command of the troops, and demoted Colonel Foster to Assistant Adjutant-General. He made Lieutenant-Colonel Brooke Young of the 6th Gore Regiment his brigade major of militia. The Black companies commanded by Captains Thomas Runchey and James Sears were posted to Chippawa. Because Colonel Cameron had fallen ill, Arthur removed him from the command of the incorporated and embodied militia on the Niagara frontier and gave that post to Colonel Kerby. [6]

Some of the incorporated militia had never been paid at all and Arthur arranged with Sir John Colborne for an expanded military chest at Kingston, with specie (coins) forwarded to Toronto for distribution on the frontiers. The rates of pay, per day, for the militia were the same as for the regulars, and made in local currency, not necessarily in coins. Local currency was worth less than Sterling:

Rate Per Day	Sterling £ s d	Currency £ s d
Lieutenant-Colonel	17. 0	19. 7
Major	16. 0	18. 5
Captain	11. 7	15. 4
Lieutenant	6. 7	7. 6
Ensign	5. 3	6. 1
Paymaster	12. 6	14. 5
Quartermaster	6. 6	7. 6
Surgeon	13. 0	15. 0
Command Pay	3. 0	3. 6
Sergeant-Major	3. 0	3. 6
Sergeant	1. 10	2. 1
Corporal	1. 4	1. 6
Private (in lieu of $8 per month)	0. 0	1. 4
Buglers	1. 1 3/4	1. 4

(According to this listing, privates were paid in local currency rather than Sterling.) Colborne agreed to appoint commissariat officers to proceed to Hamilton, London, Sandwich and Amherstburg to settle the outstanding accounts. [7]

No money was to be issued except where a proper pay list had been kept and signed by a senior military officer on the spot. Colborne wanted the magistrates to arrange for the troops' billets by using a written order addressed to a householder. A soldier's daily ration was one pound of bread or biscuit, and one pound of fresh or salt meat, and when marching under fatigue, one third of a pint of spirits. Where there was no magazine or post, militia on the march could be supplied with a sum in lieu of a daily ration, including fuel and light, not to exceed one shilling and sixpence currency per day per man, five shillings currency for an officer or one shilling and ninepence for a horse. Apparently the preceding had been implemented only haphazardly before Arthur arrived.

Soon after Arthur reached Toronto, three regiments of regulars were on duty in Upper Canada. The other four companies of the 83rd reached Kingston, where they were to be stationed. The two companies that had been sent to London with Lieutenant-Colonel Maitland were at Amherstburg, despite Colborne's wish that regulars be kept together inland. Yet Arthur felt that the militia along the Detroit frontier needed professional support. The monthly return

The execution of Samuel Lount and Peter Matthews, 12 April 1838. The scaffold stood in the courthouse yard, on the northeast corner of King and Toronto Streets, behind 66 King Street East.

dated 1 June showed that the 24th, 32nd and 83rd Regiments were all below strength. The rank and file in each stood at about 400 men.[8]

Arthur was unhappy with the arrangements for supplying his far-flung command. Commissary officers were on duty at all his posts, but the commissariat, ordnance and quartermaster's departments were in Quebec City, and he felt vulnerable so far from headquarters. His letters suggest that he wanted his own command, since communicating with Colborne, even when he was in Montreal, took too much time. In particular, Arthur felt that Upper Canada should be a separate commissariat, for most of the food his troops would need could be purchased locally, incidentally assisting the province's farmers. The system of sending accounts to headquarters for approval was inefficient. However, most of his suggestions were ignored by Colborne and the officers in Quebec City.

Arthur sent officers to inspect Upper Canada's defences, and he resolved to use some of the incorporated militia to strengthen the various fortifications, which were in deplorable condition. He moved Colonel Joseph Hill and his Queen's Light Infantry from Niagara to Sandwich, which lay open to attack and had hardly any fortifications.[9] Other militiamen would work on Fort Malden at Amherstburg, and Fort Mississauga at Niagara. Arthur then arranged with Colborne to station unattached regular officers at strategic places, as liaison men to help train the militia. Colborne assigned Major Lewis Carmichael to Coteau-du-Lac, which although in Lower Canada, was a vital spot on the supply line to Upper Canada. Other officers were posted to Cornwall, Kingston, Carillon on the Ottawa River, Prescott, and the Niagara frontier.[10]

Decent accommodation for the troops was a pressing problem. Many had been ill during the winter owing to poor housing. Smallpox had broken out in one of the companies of the Queen's Own that had been at Point Abino, while officers complained that men had suffered diseases related to exposure and overcrowding. Arthur made plans for barracks at London, Chatham, Amherstburg and Drummondville; Kingston alone was well served. Even Toronto's Fort York was too cramped, and many troops were billetted in the city.

An existing blockhouse at Gananoque, built in 1813, could be repaired, but others were needed at Brockville, at Kingston Mills, Jones Falls and the Whitefish dam on the Rideau system, as well as on Bois Blanc Island in the Detroit River. The only blockhouses along the Rideau were at Merrickville and Newboro (The Isthmus). That route was vital for the movement of supplies, since it was safer from attack than the St. Lawrence. Many of the structures Arthur planned would be built in the succeeding months.[11]

He appointed Andrew Drew his Commodore of the Provincial Marine, with John Elmsley as one of his captains, and he reopened the dockyard at Kingston. He leased the steamers *Cobourg, Queen Victoria*, and *William IV*, and purchased the steamers *Toronto* and *Experiment*, and all were armed.[12] In deference to a clause of the Rush-Bagot Agreement of 1818 that allowed only one vessel on Lake Ontario from each country to carry an 18-pounder gun, only the steamer *Experiment* carried such a weapon. Two officers of the Royal Navy, Captain Williams Sandom and Lieutenant William Fowell, arrived from Quebec City with 200 sailors and Royal Marines for the naval service.

Early in May, Major Robert Anstruther, the unattached officer stationed on the Niagara frontier, reported on conditions there. He was pleased with Colonel Kerby's work, and that of his subordinate, Lieutenant-Colonel John Clark at Niagara, (who had taken command of the Frontier Light Infantry when Colonel Cameron was unable to carry on), and with Major Ogden Creighton's cavalry, and he repeated Kerby's request that a detachment of Major Magrath's Queen's Lancers, then in the London District, be sent to Niagara. Skimping on cavalry might prove an unwise economy.

The incorporated militiamen were not always well behaved. Two companies of the Frontier Light Infantry were moved from Niagara to Drummondville because they were unruly. Kerby had to cope with drunkenness and fights in the Queen's Niagara Fencibles. Some Roman Catholics, eager to demonstrate their loyalty, had enlisted, but the Orangemen in the regiment could not resist baiting them.

In May, Arthur went to inspect the troops on the Niagara frontier. Suspicious characters had been seen near St. David's, and Arthur had Major Creighton send four companies of the Frontier Light Infantry to scour that area and the Short Hills, to the south of St. Catharines. They found nothing out of the ordinary, and Arthur returned to Toronto.[13]

Meanwhile, the "pirate", Bill Johnston, from one of his Fort Wallaces in the Thousand Islands, was planning an outrage. This hideout was believed to be a secluded spot on Abel's Island, at the head of Wellesley Island, the largest in the group. In Clayton, Johnston boasted openly that he had 150 to 200 men, and he intended acting against Kingston, unfettered by the presence of

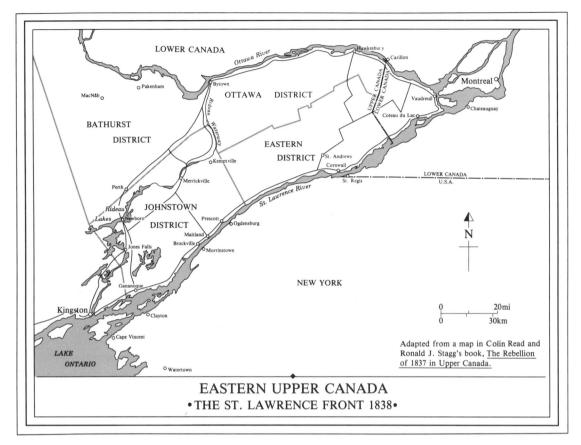

LOWER CANADA

Ottawa River

Pakenham

MacNab

BATHURST

DISTRICT

Bytown

OTTAWA   DISTRICT

Rideau Waterway

Perth

Kemptville

Merrickville

EASTERN

DISTRICT

St. Andrews

Cornwall

St. Lawrence River

St. Regis

LOWER CANADA

U.S.A.

Rideau

Lakes

Newboro

JOHNSTOWN

DISTRICT

Prescott

Maitland

Brockville

Jones Falls

Morrinstown

Ogdensburg

Gananoque

Kingston

Clayton

Cape Vincent

LAKE

ONTARIO

Watertown

Hawkesbury

Carillon

Montreal

Vaudreuil

Coteau du Lac

Chateauguay

UPPER CANADA

LOWER CANADA

NEW YORK

N

0   20mi

0   30km

Adapted from a map in Colin Read and
Ronald J. Stagg's book, The Rebellion
of 1837 in Upper Canada.

EASTERN UPPER CANADA
• THE ST. LAWRENCE FRONT 1838 •

Rensselaer Van Rensselaer. Swaggering through the village, Johnston sported two rifled pistols and a bowie knife at his belt. The archipelago afforded the perfect setting for piracy, and was well known as a spot that harboured ne'er-do-wells. Many of the islands were rocky and did not attract farmers, and enough brigands and smugglers hid there with their own boats to endanger the St. Lawrence route to the interior. Canadian rebels had also sought shelter there. Valuable upbound shipping used the Rideau Canal when the shallow locks were not frozen, although steamers often ran down the St. Lawrence, shooting the rapids to save time. Other steamers operated between Kingston and Prescott, serving communities along the shore. One such was the *Sir Robert Peel*, owned by a syndicate in Brockville.

Pirate Bill's light-weight row galley was some forty feet long,

and his gang, which Donald McLeod had joined after the episode at Fighting Island, amounted to hardly more than twenty men. He knew the *Peel*'s schedule when he took his followers to Wellesley Island on the evening of 29 May. The island is indented by a deep, narrow bay known as Lake-of-the-Isles. Wood-burning steamers had to stop frequently for the bulky fuel, and one station was on Wellesley Island a short distance inside the lake. At that point the north shore of the lake is formed by Hill Island. In 1838 a shanty stood next to a wharf that was piled with small logs.

On duty at midnight was a man named Ripley, whose home was on Abel's Island. Ripley's suspicions were aroused, since Johnston was incapable of doing anything quietly, when he saw a long boat full of men passing the entrance to the lake more than once. Now he heard someone shout, "She's coming!" as the *Peel* moved through the narrows. Ripley warned her captain, John Armstrong, that strangers were lurking as the steamer, bound for Kingston, drew in at the wharf. Aboard were some thirty cabin passengers and forty in the steerage, but Captain Armstrong did not take the words of caution seriously. The crew came ashore to carry on the wood, a task not finished until 2.00 a.m. on the morning of the 30th. Suddenly, from the woods, a number of well-armed men appeared, dressed and painted as Indians. While part of the force blocked the gang plank to prevent the crew reaching the ship, others roused the passengers and herded them onto the wharf. Bill Johnston and a few others aboard the *Peel* cut her loose, while the rest of the gang followed in three small boats they had previously concealed on the shore. Johnston tried to start the *Peel*'s engine. He did not succeed before she grounded probably on a shoal. His shout, "Revenge for the *Caroline*! Remember the *Caroline*!" echoed through the boats as the men aboard the *Peel* set her afire. Unknown to the thieves, Roderick McSwain, the mate and pilot, was asleep in his cabin. The brigands took off in their boats and McSwain, badly burnt, swam to and one passenger had been carrying about £1,300 in bank notes. Johnston's men robbed Colonel Richard Duncan Fraser, the commander of the 2nd Grenville Regiment, of £300.

Sir George Arthur issued a proclamation pleading that Canadians should not retaliate, and on 2 June the new governor general, Lord Durham, offered a reward of $1,000 for information that would lead to the conviction of any of Johnston's gang. Durham had only been ashore in Quebec City a few days when the news of the *Peel* reached him. William Marcy, the governor of New York State, posted rewards of $500 for Johnston, $250 each for Samuel C. Frey, Donald McLeod and Robert Smith, and $100 for each of the others. Marcy went to Clayton and stayed some days, gathering information. President Van Buren ordered a reinforcement of troops for Sackets Harbor, and an armed steamer to patrol the area. Nine men were arrested. and identified by Dr. Thomas Scott, who had been a passenger on the *Peel*. Only one, William Anderson, was tried, and he was acquitted by a friendly jury. [15]

Johnston remained at large amidst rumours as to his presence along the river. He was reported near Brockville, and then at Oak Point, seven miles upriver on the American side. He also plundered

William "Bill" Johnston, treasured in Clayton, New York as the "Pirate of the St. Lawrence". The original is in B.J. Lossing's *The Pictorial Field-Book of the War of 1812* .

the wharf.[14]

Captain Armstrong borrowed a skiff from Ripley and rowed to Gananoque, hired a fast horse and galloped to Kingston for help. His news had the opposite effect, for the authorities ordered all steamers to stay in port. After huddling in the shanty on Wellesley Island for some hours, the *Peel*'s passengers, many in their night clothes, were rescued when the United States steamer *Oneida* stopped, and delivered them to Kingston.

Contemporary accounts vary. One recorded that the *Peel* carried £20,000 in specie to pay the troops, but such a large sum would have been transported along the Rideau Canal at that time of year. Yet the losses were substantial for the ship was valued at $11,000

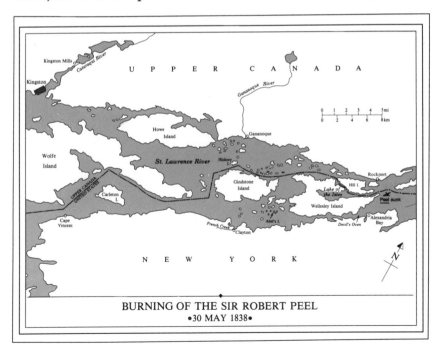

BURNING OF THE SIR ROBERT PEEL
•30 MAY 1838•

homes on Amherst Island early in June. On the 28th, "General" James Phillips, formerly of Bastard Township, Leeds County, crossed the St. Lawrence east of Gananoque with a party of men, intending to attack locks along the Rideau Canal. Their presence was discovered, and some of the 2nd Leeds Regiment turned out. Ogle Gowan, the Orange leader and a captain in the regiment, recorded that Phillips' pursuers were led by a Mr. Macdonell, a Roman Catholic. (Gowan occasionally weakened his position as Grand Master by courting Catholic votes.) The searchers could not find Phillips, but they captured one John Thomas and took him to Brockville. [16]

That month the 34th (Cumberland) Regiment arrived in Upper

Jones Falls on the Rideau ca. 1838, watercolour by Philip J. Bainbrigge. The many red coats in the original suggest that the boats shown were carrying troops.

Canada, under the command of Major (soon to be Lieutenant-Colonel) Richard Airey. The regiment travelled by way of the Rideau Canal and Airey set up a temporary headquarters at the Merrickville blockhouse. With the rank and file numbering 535, the 34th was the first full-strength battalion to reach the province. The 24th and 32nd Regiments had been in Canada before the rebellions, but like the 83rd, the 34th (and the 43rd that would come later) were moved from the Maritimes. The returns for the 34th and 43rd shed light on the presence of women and children. For generations a quota of wives had been part of a regiment, to do the housekeeping.

If they had children, they, too, travelled with the troops. Their living conditions were sometimes appalling, for they slept wherever they could find a spot, often on bare floors.

The distribution return shows where all the regulars in Upper Canada were stationed on 1 June 1838. Apart from the troops at the regimental headquarters, half a company of the 24th was at Carillon on the Ottawa River. Part of the 34th was in transit along the Rideau Canal en route to Amherstburg while three companies had reached Toronto. One company of the 32nd was at Simcoe, and a small detachment of the 32nd and two companies of the 83rd were at Amherstburg. Part of the company of the 24th was at Penetanguishene. [17]

Like the women and children of the regulars, families of some men serving in incorporated militia regiments also resided at each regimental headquarters, but were not always not provided with rations as were the families of regulars. Colonel James Kerby established a school for the children of his Queen's Niagara Fencibles at Fort Erie. Women and children accompanied Colonel Joseph Hill's Queen's Light Infantry from Toronto to Niagara in January 1838. When Hill's regiment was moved to Sandwich in March, some of the families were left behind. On 20 April, Kerby informed the office of the Adjutant-General of Militia that these women and children were in a destitute condition. In response, Lieutenant-Colonel Maitland, in command of the London and Western Districts, discharged the men whose families at Niagara needed them. [18]

Captain (left) and private (right) in the 85th Regiment. The 85th was dispatched in horse sleighs from New Brunswick to Lower Canada in 1837, and was sent on to Upper Canada in 1838

Merrickville on the Rideau, watercolour by Philip J. Bainbrigge, showing the blockhouse overlooking the locks. Part of the 34th Regiment stopped for a time at the blockhouse while in transit from Montreal to Amherstburg in 1838.

Sandwich in the 1830s. During the rebellions Sandwich was a distinct community. Now it is part of greater Windsor.

View of Prescott in October 1830 by Thomas Burrowes. Prescott was a busy forwarding port. Fort Wellington stood just east of the village.

Chapter 9
The Short Hills, June 1838

All through the spring, Colonel Kerby and Major Anstruther had been worried that insurgents might take up a position in the Short Hills, in Pelham Township, because of the sympathies of the nearby inhabitants, and the nature of the terrain. As in Norwich, in the London District, many people were Quakers. The Short Hills made a perfect hideout, a very broken, wild area, through which a rough track led north towards St. Catharines. At that spot a large indent pierces the Niagara Escarpment, an enormous notch that was filled with hummocky glacial debris at the close of the last ice age. Kerby, a local man, knew that dislodging a hostile force from these hills would be difficult, and Major Anstruther agreed with him.

Reporting early in May, Anstruther was alarmed at the number of easy crossing points between Niagara and Fort Erie. The only secure zone lay along the Niagara gorge, a natural barrier. Invaders could land and reach the Short Hills "well known as the strongest position in the district", before the troops at Drummondville and Fort Erie could hear of the crossing. The incorporated militia had been reduced through discharges, and Anstruther recommended in particular, increasing the number of cavalry patrolling from Niagara to Queenston, and from above the Falls to Fort Erie. [1]

Feeling ran high among the republicans in Buffalo. They were mourning the executions of Matthews and Lount, and talking of an invasion to release six of Duncombe's rebels who were being held in Hamilton under sentence of death. While much of the initiative for raids on Upper Canada was passing into the hands of Americans, Canadians were not prepared to give up all part. Canadians in exile had formed the Canadian Refugee Association, led by the unpredictable Dr. A.K. Mackenzie of Hamilton, with headquarters in Lockport, New York. Dr. Charles Duncombe was a charter member. [2]

Some republicans who had enrolled for an expedition against Hamilton infiltrated the town by 18 April. While there they learned that the sentences of the condemned men had been commuted to prison terms or transportation to a penal colony. Returning to the American side, they reported that Hamilton was swarming with militiamen. On 2 June, Major Henry Dive Townshend of the 24th Regiment arrived at Drummondville to take command of all the troops on the Niagara frontier, relieving Colonel Kerby, who would continue on duty at Fort Erie. Townshend remained a major in the British army and in his regiment, but he was given local rank of lieutenant-colonel. This accounts for the discrepancy between the official reports and the Army List. [3]

On 4 June, as usual, militia colonels across the province reviewed their sedentary members. Colonel Samuel Street's 3rd Lincoln Regiment, from the townships of Willoughby, Bertie, Crowland, Humberstone and Wainfleet, mustered at Chippawa. Colonel Kerby's 2nd Lincolns, from the townships of Stamford, Thorold and Pelham, gathered at Allanburg, on the Welland Canal. At each place some 800 militiamen turned out, but Street reported that his men possessed only forty-three muskets. Kerby had been worried that the men of Pelham might hold back, but he found no evidence that any had stayed home.

The following day, two companies of the 34th Regiment reached Drummondville, and Lieutenant-Colonel Townshend asked Kerby to find accommodation for them. They had to use tents temporarily, for the only available houses were close to the canal, where regulars would be tempted to desert. More incorporated militia were required on the Niagara frontier, and the rest of William Kingsmill's Queen's Own was moved from Toronto to reinforce the Frontier Light Infantry and Queen's Niagara Fencibles, the two Black companies at Chippawa and the few regulars.

This show of strength, duly relayed to the republicans across the water, obviously did not deter them as they were boasting that they could assemble 500 men, and had hidden 1,200 small arms and six cannon. The United States regulars in the area numbered scarcely ninety men. On 6 June at Niagara, Lieutenant-Colonel John Clark received three American visitors — Major Nathaniel Young, a regular officer, Captain Romans of the United States Navy, and Mr. G.W. Clinton, the collector of customs at Buffalo. They hoped to stop further depredations, and Young assured Clark that he was expecting reinforcements shortly. The next day, to Kerby's satisfaction, Major Thomas Magrath arrived from Brantford at the head of his Queen's Lancers. Small patrols spread out from Point Abino on Lake Erie to Niagara. [4]

That same night of 7 June, 200 republicans led by George Washington Case, a Duncombe rebel, and James Morreau, an Irish Roman Catholic from Pennsylvania, marched through Lewiston for Clark's Point, below the Falls. Some open boats were waiting and their objective was Queenston, where Captain Lewis Palmer was stationed with his company of Frontier Light Infantry. From Queenston the republicans intended seizing Forts George and Mississauga at Niagara. As usual they showed more bark than bite,

for only twenty-three of them embarked, and the entire force of 200 fled when they discovered that some American regulars were approaching. Then fifty of the regulars took post at a nearby landing to forestall further attempts to effect a crossing. Despite American vigilance, on 10 June twenty-nine republicans, the majority of them Canadian exiles, crossed on the steamer *Red Jacket* to Grand Island, where they obtained fifty to sixty small arms and some ammunition. They landed above Chippawa, moved inland, and set up camp in a tamarack swamp in Willoughby Township. Some of them slept at Rice's nearby tavern.

In the party were Alexander McLeod and John James McNulty, both suspected of having been with Mackenzie at Montgomery's Tavern, Benjamin Wait, who had visited Navy Island, Jacob Beamer, one of Duncombe's rebels, and Samuel Chandler, who had a list (possibly forged) of 526 men in Pelham Township who had enrolled in the cause. Chandler was to be the commissary, while the man held responsible for initiating the enterprise was James Morreau. Only three days after the aborted attempt to reach Queenston, Morreau was ready for more action. [5] They obtained bread from a friend in Chippawa, then the twenty-nine broke into small groups, and on the 11th all headed for the Short Hills, about fifteen miles distant. There they expected to be joined by large numbers of disaffected Canadians.

Some of the intruders found shelter in a barn belonging to Lewis Wilson, who had left the province, but two women of the household supplied them with food, then and later. On the 12th the men took up a position in the Short Hills, three miles west of the village of St. Johns, where they had a good view in all directions, and enough cover to conceal their presence. They sent a message to "Major-General" Daniel McLeod, now the commander of the "Patriot Army of the North-west", who was in Lockport, asking him for instructions from the "Provisional Government". McLeod sent his aide-de-camp, Linus Miller, to order the men, now more than thirty strong for some local supporters

The home of James and Laura Secord at Chippawa. The heroine of the War of 1812 and her husband, a veteran of that war, were living in Chippawa when the rebellions broke out.

Thomas Magrath, commander of the Queen's Lancers. An enthusiastic sportsman, Magrath was Commodore of the Royal Canadian Yacht Club in 1854 and 1855.

warned of the intruders' arrival. He sent Lieutenant James Magrath (the major's younger brother), Cornet Charles Heath, Sergeant Robert Bailey, a corporal and ten troopers of the Queen's Lancers, to St. Johns to keep watch and scout the area.

Writing to Sir John Colborne from Toronto on 17 June, Sir George Arthur informed him that he had asked Lieutenant-Colonel Townshend to state what force he required to protect the Niagara frontier. Townshend had replied that the American authorities knew of men congregating and plotting something. Townshend had 900 men under arms, but he felt that twice this number would be desirable, for security and to inspire confidence among the loyal populace. He recommended incorporating four new militia regiments of from 400 to 500 men each. Ogden Creighton, recently promoted to lieutenant-colonel in command of the Black companies at Chippawa, had informed Townshend that a few brigands had reached Grand Island, and that some might already be in the province.

Arthur told Colborne that Major Richard Webbe, of the Queen's Niagara Fencibles, had been rudely treated the week before while visiting Buffalo to dine with a friend. Webbe was mobbed and forced to "decamp by the railroad dinnerless." The American authorities felt compelled to condemn this rowdiness because Major Nathaniel Young, the American regular officer, complained. Webbe and Young were good friends. At a special inquest, the jurors expressed their disapproval, but seemed powerless to take action. Arthur requested more arms — 10,000 for Kingston, 5,000 each for Toronto and the Western District, as well as carriages for his 6-pounder guns, bedsteads, blankets and barrack furniture. He had asked Major Richard Bonnycastle to come to Toronto to oversee the construction of new barracks, and Captain Williams Sandom to improve the naval force on Lake Erie. [7]

Three companies of the 85th (King's Light Infantry) Regiment had reached Kingston, by steamers along the St. Lawrence, and Arthur was expecting the other three shortly. The commander was Lieutenant-Colonel Frederick Maunsell. Blue facings denoted a Royal regiment, an honour granted the unit in 1821. [8]

Although few Canadians had joined him at his hideout in the Short Hills, James Morreau told Linus Miller that he had no intention of returning to American soil until he had struck a blow for liberty. Morreau gave up his command, though, probably because he was now uncertain of the success of the expedition. As the days passed, the invaders' whereabouts remained a mystery to the

had joined them, to return at once. The general was planning a large-scale operation for 4 July to celebrate American independence, and he did not want the Canadian authorities alerted. Morreau ignored the summons. Local people continued supplying food, but most refused to commit themselves unless Morreau received the 500 reinforcements which he claimed were on their way. [6]

Reports reaching Chippawa told of strangers in the neighbourhood, and Magistrate James Cummings sent a search party to Willoughby Township. The men found the camp in the tamarack swamp, and because they found the remains of four fires they concluded that perhaps forty or fifty men had been there. On 12 June, Lieutenant-Colonel Townshend, at Drummondville, was military. They were joined by half a dozen men from across the border, and enough Canadians to bring their force to between forty and seventy men — the sole occasion when republican intruders would draw much local support. Morreau felt reassured, because the men who had come from New York State had reported that Major-General Daniel McLeod was following them with 300 "patriots". On the evening of 20 June, Morreau and the other acknowledged leader, Jacob Beamer, decided to attack the detachment of Queen's Lancers that were known to be staying at Osterhout's tavern in St. Johns.

The men divided into three groups, to approach the village from three directions to prevent anyone escaping and spreading the alarm. Beamer left at 9.00 p.m. with the first group; Morreau followed at 11.00 p.m. with the second. He caught up with Beamer, who had stopped to rob the home of ninety-year-old Abraham Overholt, a former German soldier who had served under General John Burgoyne in 1777, and later in Butler's Rangers. Beamer's men stole $1,000 from Overholt, and $300 from his son Martin before moving towards St. Johns. [9] The third group under Alexander Mcleod joined them, and at 2.00 a.m. on 21 June they surrounded Osterhout's tavern. Asleep inside were Sergeant Bailey, the corporal and ten lancers; Lieutenant Magrath and Cornet Heath were elsewhere. [10]

After barricading the doors and windows downstairs, the lancers began firing their pistols at the attackers from the upper storey. After half an hour of stalemate, Morreau's men brought bales of straw to set fire to the tavern. At that Bailey agreed to surrender. As dawn broke the raiders marched the lancers into the woods, where they argued over what to do with their prisoners. Beamer and Chandler favoured hanging seven on the spot, but Morreau and Miller objected. They settled on taking the lancers' arms — pistols and swords; they had no lances — and releasing them after they gave their paroles not to oppose any republicans in future. Word of the attack was carried to Chippawa and on to Drummondville, and the militia responded. The incorporated men began a search, while Lieutenant-Colonel Andrew Roraback of the 2nd Lincoln Regiment embodied some of the infantry and Captain John McMicking's company of cavalry. Amidst exaggerated reports — the lancers thought that 100 men had attacked them — the hunt was on. Lieutenant Magrath returned to St Johns, while Cornet Heath, riding there, spotted Samuel Chandler and gave chase. Chandler entered a swamp, and when Heath's horse sank deeply into the mire, he hopped off, followed on foot, subdued Chandler and arrested him. [11]

Lieutenant-Colonel Roraback organized more than four companies to scour the neighbourhood, while McMicking's cavalrymen took post at various crossroads. Sixty infantrymen went into the woods, and one company of the militia went with Roraback to St. Johns. One company backtracked to the camp in the tamarack swamp in Willoughby Township where the brigands had stopped after they landed. One company went to Misener's bridge over the Chippawa River, while the last occupied Rice's tavern and the approaches to it. With the escape route to the Niagara River so well guarded, many of the marauders tried to get across the Grand River and into the London District where they could expect to find friends.

On 22 June, obeying a directive originating with Sir John Colborne, Adjutant-General of Militia Richard Bullock issued a Militia General Order to reduce the size of the incorporated regiments — the Queen's Rangers, Queen's Light Infantry, Royal Foresters, Frontier Light Infantry, Queen's Niagara Fencibles and Queen's Own Regiment of Militia. As of 1 July, each regiment would consist of six companies instead of ten, but the services of those who were discharged would be extended until 31 July.[12] Colborne's instructions to Bullock had been in transit when Arthur wrote his letter of 17 July to inform the commander of forces of the need to add more incorporated units. No wonder Arthur felt that he needed more independence from headquarters.

With rumours of a large scale invasion circulating in Upper Canada, Arthur wanted the raid and the raiders dealt with swiftly and with maximum force in order to deter further invaders. He issued a proclamation that no one was to enter or leave the province without a passport, and he ordered Colonel Sir Allan MacNab to call out two of the Gore regiments. Then Arthur asked Samuel Peters Jarvis, in his capacity as Superintendent of Indian Affairs, to relay an order to William Johnson Kerr at Wellington Square to call out some warriors. A detachment was needed to guard the bridge over the Grand River, and Kerr was to bring a party to the Niagara frontier. Afterwards Arthur set out by steamer for Hamilton, accompanied by the solicitor-general, William Henry Draper.

The Indians responded quickly, and by the time Kerr reached the mouth of the Grand River he had 300 with him. Before leaving he sent another 100 men to Oakland Township to scare the disaffected in that area. From the Grand he led his 300 warriors east and into the Short Hills, but they did not capture any of the republicans.[13]

In the London District, Colonel George W. Whitehead of the 1st Oxford Regiment called out sixty-five men, and together with eighty

Indians they began hunting for escapers. His force soon swelled to some 500 volunteers, inspired by fear of another outbreak of rebellion in the district.

From Hamilton, Arthur issued a further proclamation offering a reward of $250 for the capture of James Morreau. Men of the 4th Lincoln Regiment apprehended Morreau, Beamer, McLeod, Wait and McNulty in Gainsborough Township, west of Pelham. All told, thirty-nine men were arrested, as were the two women at Lewis Wilson's farm who had supplied the invaders with food. Most of the

prisoners were moved to Toronto, but the ringleaders would be taken to Niagara later to stand trial in the district where the outrage had been committed. Between the Hickory Island incursion and that of the Short Hills, there had been little participation by Canadians. Afterwards, Canadians played even less a part in the raids.

Arthur rode to Drummondville, arriving on the evening of the 23 June. More rumours circulated, and at Fort Erie Colonel Kerby had been in communication with Major Nathaniel Young in Buffalo, who was trying to curb the republicans. In the spring and early summer the self-styled General of the "Patriot Army of the Northwest", Henry Handy, was busily forming a secret organization, "the Secret Order of the Sons of Liberty" along the western border. He hoped to create an underground army linked by secret agents reporting to him with the intention of invading Canada on 4 July and rousing the populace to join him. A rival organization being formed in June at Cleveland was also planning a July invasion.[14] Major Young warned Kerby that Iroquois Indians in New York State had gathered at Buffalo, which might have serious consequences if they joined their brethren in Upper Canada. Also, the raiders' motive in going to the Short Hills had been to stir up the Indians. Young's suspicions revealed how little Americans understood the Indians in British territory. Far from rising against the government, they were among its staunchest supporters. [15]

The courthouse at Niagara where James Morreau was tried and executed for his part in the Short Hills raid. The building is now the Court House Theatre and part of the annual Shaw Festival at Niagara-on-the-Lake.

Major Young later called on Sir George Arthur at Drummondville, to assure him that he wanted to cooperate in stopping further republican landings. On the 24th, Arthur rode through the area where the raiders had been hidden, accompanied by an escort of Queen's Lancers. He found militia volunteers still searching for raiders and the people who had helped them, and concluded that not more than 100 people had been involved. Yet he viewed the situation gravely. Many "lawless characters" had been moving to the American frontier in recent years, and abetted by Canadian refugees they would cause more border troubles. [16]

Arthur sent three companies of the 24th Regiment from Toronto to Drummondville, and ordered a half-battery of artillery to be moved from Kingston. The reductions in the incorporated regiments were carried out, as ordered by Colborne, and were welcomed by the men who were anxious to resume civilian life, their farms having been neglected after six months of service. Lieutenant-Colonel Townshend was worried that the reductions would serve as a signal for more crossings, but Arthur hoped that the extra regulars would be a deterrent. He returned to Toronto on 29 June, where more disturbing news awaited him.

From London, Lieutenant-Colonel Maitland reported three crossings by republicans along the St. Clair River. Some forty had landed at Sarnia and looted a store and a house before a party of local Indians drove them back to Michigan. Others crossed and were near Delaware before the militia rallied and put them to flight. Captain John Elmsley, now in command of a gunboat on Lake Erie, apprehended six of the men who had tried to reach Delaware. A sloop had landed republicans at Goderich, who robbed some stores before they sailed away. The American steamer *Governor Marcy* captured six of the raiders. Maitland also suspected that the republicans planned to attack the base at Penetanguishene.

Arthur ordered three gunboats and the steamer *Toronto* through the Welland Canal to reinforce Elmsley. Meanwhile, Major-General John Clitherow, the commander at Montreal, took action when he heard of the Short Hills raid. Without waiting for orders from Sir John Colborne, he dispatched the 43rd (Monmouthshire Light Infantry) Regiment to Upper Canada. The first companies, and the commander, Lieutenant-Colonel Henry Booth, reached Kingston on 2 July. In a letter to Sir Allan MacNab, Arthur called the 43rd "one of the finest in the British Army." [17]

The half-battery arrived from Kingston at Toronto on 4 July, but Arthur returned it since the alarm seemed over. Colborne sent Colonel Charles Chichester, an unattached officer, to the London District to help train the militia.

The Delaware, or Moravian, Indian village on the Thames River, by Philip J. Bainbrigge. Local Reformers were afraid that the Indians, encouraged by government supporters, would attack them.

On the 8th, Arthur ordered Colonel Samuel Peters Jarvis to move his Queen's Rangers from Toronto to the Niagara frontier. The lieutenant governor then received word that Sir John Colborne was coming to Upper Canada to see the situation at first hand. [18]

Old Sly's Locks on the Rideau waterway southeast of Smiths Falls. Completed in 1832, the waterway, a safe alternative route to the St. Lawrence, was used briefly for military purposes during the rebellion era. Artist Thomas Burrowes' watercolours are a valuable record of the 1830s.

Captain (left) and private (right) of the 43rd Regiment of Foot. The regiment was dispatched to Upper Canada following the Short Hills raid and stationed on the Niagara frontier.

Chapter 10
A Viceregal Visit and a Reinforcement

John George Lambton, 1st Earl of Durham, Governor General of Canada, 1838-1839, author of the famous report. Durham visited Upper Canada for a week in July 1838.

On 25 June 1838 Sir John Colborne ordered Major Bonnycastle to establish a line of posts along the St. Lawrence, the Niagara, and the shores of the London and Western Districts. (Bonnycastle was now Sir Richard, knighted for his services at Kingston.) At the same time, Colborne admitted that attempting to protect the shore all the way from the St. Clair River to Fort Erie would be unwise. To do so would mean placing troops in such small detachments that each would be vulnerable if attacked in force. Therefore he decided to strengthen his naval service. Perhaps he was aware of the Duke of Wellington's advice in 1814, "that superiority on the lakes is a sine qua non of success in war on the frontier of Canada, even if our object should be only defensive". [1]

Colborne wanted Captain Williams Sandom to order two schooners to Long Point and to hire another steamboat for Lake Erie. Two more steamers were already being fitted out at Kingston for use among the Thousand Islands, but both would be armed with light guns, to avoid challenging the Americans over the Rush-Bagot Agreement of 1818. The 18-pounder mounted on the steamer *Experiment* filled Britain's quota.

In the same letter Colborne recommended that companies of volunteers be organized under "Officers of the Line" for the Detroit and Niagara fronts, and for Prescott and Cornwall. The three companies of the 85th Regiment and most of the 34th had now reached Toronto, and Colborne hoped that Arthur could soon send three companies of the 24th to Kingston. That regiment had been on "hard duty" and should be sent to Quebec to be refitted. Sir John was dispatching Lieutenant-Colonel William Cox, an unattached officer, to replace Major Robert Anstruther on the Niagara frontier, and he wanted Lieutenant-Colonel Townshend to rejoin the 24th Regiment where he was needed. [2]

Colborne approved Major-General Clitherow's action in sending Arthur the 43rd Regiment, which reached Niagara on 10 July. By that time Sir John himself had left for the upper province with more reinforcements. These were a "company" of the Royal Artillery, and what were described on the War Office return as "two companies" of the lst (King's) Dragoon Guards in the scarlet faced blue of a Royal regiment. Colborne was followed by the new governor general, Lord Durham, with a suitable entourage. Durham reached Kingston on 11 July, and Sir George Arthur received him in Toronto the following day. Durham recommended abolishing the legislative council since that body was unrepresentative — an anathema to the governor general who was nicknamed "Radical Jack" for his liberal views. Arthur refused because such a move would be unconstitutional, and involve him with the "Provincial Parliament." [3] Durham took a steamer to Queenston on the 13th. Colborne met him and they rode to Niagara where the 43rd Regiment was encamped.

On the 10th, Colborne had decreed that the incorporated militia be discharged, now that more regulars were in the province. Most of the men were pleased, for they had been distressed at the prospect of serving until the end of the month.[4] The regiments that had performed the hardest service were Cameron's Frontier Light Infantry, Kerby's Queen's Niagara Fencibles, Hill's Queen's Light Infantry, and Kingsmill's Queen's Own. Jarvis' Queen's Rangers had garrisoned Toronto, except for the few days when the regiment went to Queenston to search for weapons among the civilians. Carthew's Royal Foresters also stayed in Toronto, although a detachment had marched to Newmarket in February to search for weapons among the civilians. [5]

Lord Durham spent hardly a week in Upper Canada, but he deliberately courted publicity in the United States as a way of discouraging further depredations. If the American authorities were too weak, or disinterested, to control the brigands, a show of British force might work. On the evening of 13 July, Arthur arrived from Toronto, and Durham agreed to review the regulars at Niagara on Tuesday, the 17th, at 10.00 a.m. The governor general set up headquarters at the Falls near Drummondville on the 14th, and

rode to Chippawa and Fort Erie. At Fort Erie he found Colonel Kerby completing arrangements for the discharge of the Queen's Niagara Fencibles. Lieutenant-Colonel Townshend was preparing to return to the 24th Regiment, and the new commander on the Niagara frontier would be Lieutenant-Colonel Henry Booth of the 43rd. Before handing over to Booth, Townshend wrote to Major Nathaniel Young in Buffalo, inviting the Americans to attend the review of troops at Niagara.

The event was well publicized in the American newspapers, and many people crossed over to watch the splendid marchpast of the 43rd, the Dragoon Guards and Royal Artillery, and part of the 24th. Afterwards, Durham entertained several American officers, who seemed well-disposed. He attributed their attitude to the display they had witnessed. Arthur, however, expected more trouble as winter

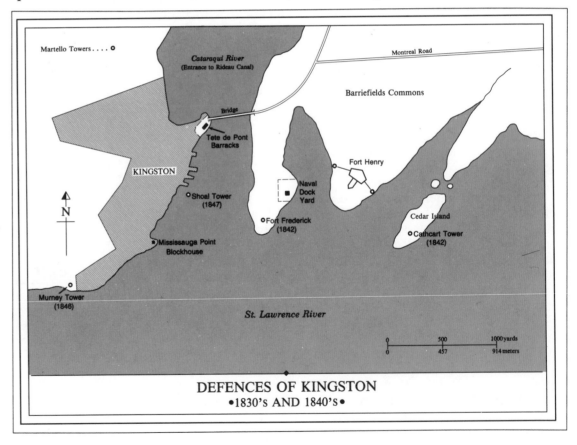

DEFENCES OF KINGSTON
•1830's AND 1840's•

approached. Unemployment rose with the arrival of cold weather, and idle republicans would cross the frontiers when the ice was firm.

On 18 July the trial of James Morreau began at Niagara, for his part in the Short Hills raid, and he was condemned to hang on the 30th. Durham advised against granting clemency. While Arthur had told Lord Glenelg that there would not be any more executions, Morreau's case was different because he was not an Upper Canadian rebel. Nor did the American authorities try to intervene, for President Van Buren stuck to his statement that citizens who indulged in outrages outside their country could not expect his protection. The execution was carried out as scheduled by the district sheriff, Alexander Hamilton. [6]

On the night of 29 July, fifteen prisoners escaped from Fort Henry — all Upper Canadian rebels sentenced to be transported to a penal colony. A sympathetic employee of the fort was thought to have supplied them with an iron bar and a spike nail, and information on the fort's layout. They loosened mortar and removed enough stones to gain access to an adjoining room, from which a passage led into the ditch between the inner and outer walls. Using a scaling ladder made of boards from their beds, they got over the outer wall and down the other side. One was John Montgomery, convicted of treason although his main crime had been the ownership of the tavern on Yonge Street. He broke his leg while dropping into the ditch and was helped over the outer wall by the others.

The escapers broke into small groups; Gilbert Morden of Lloydtown, Stephen Brophy and Walter Chase (captured on the schooner *Anne*) stayed with Montgomery. Despite Montgomery's painful leg, the four were the first to reach the American shore. They found a canoe near the road to Gananoque, paddled to Carleton Island, and from there they were taken to Farren's tavern in Cape Vincent, to a hero's welcome. Eight others joined them, but the remaining three — John G. Parker, Leonard Watson and William Stockdale — were retaken and returned to Fort Henry. [7]

At the time of the breakout Sir John Colborne was still at Niagara. On 6 August he issued more instructions for forming volunteer companies to guard the frontiers where crossings could be most easily effected. Apart from the volunteers, he felt that the militia could be reduced. Five companies of the 34th Regiment moved to Amherstburg, and after his return to Lower Canada, from Sorel on 16 August, Colborne ordered a detachment of the 34th to Sandwich. Captain Sandom was to station a gunboat and two pinnances at Windsor, for service on the Detroit and St. Clair frontier. Now that the 34th was in the Western District, he ordered the two companies of the 83rd to return to the regimental headquarters at Kingston.

He sent a company of the 71st Regiment

Men of the 71st Regiment escorting prisoners to jail in Montreal. One company of this regiment was dispatched to Brockville because of "disputes between the militia and the politicians".

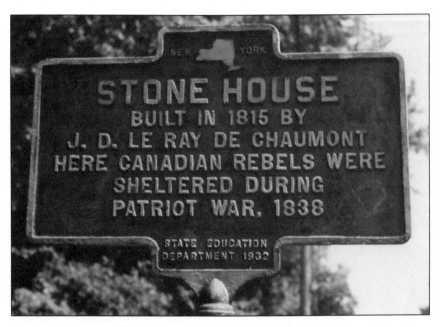

Plaque on a house in Cape Vincent, New York, commemorating the rebels who escaped from Fort Henry and succeeded in reaching the American side.

The 43rd Regiment at Niagara Falls. While stationed along the Niagara frontier, the officers of the 43rd enjoyed excursions to view the Falls.

to Brockville, where tension had been high since the winter. [8] The Reformers were offended by the aggressive loyalty of the Orangemen, under their champion, Ogle Gowan. The 71st Highland Light Infantry wore shakos that had diced bands of red-white, and — for irony — Mackenzie tartan trews. [9] Regulars from Kingston, Brockville and a few attached to the Royal Engineers at Bytown could be used to guard the Rideau Canal. A company of the Glengarry Militia then at Prescott, or any other raised, should occupy posts at Gananoque, Prescott and Cornwall. All other militia in the area was to be disembodied. [10]

At Niagara, the trials of the other Short Hills raiders began on 18 August. Twenty received the death penalty, which was remitted. Jacob Beamer, Samuel Chandler, Alexander McLeod, John James McNulty, Linus Miller and Benjamin Wait were among the men whose sentences were commuted to transportation for life; others received terms in the penitentiary at Kingston. The sentences to a penal colony were sufficiently harsh, Arthur thought, to serve as a deterrent to other republicans planning border crossings. [11]

By September, however, Arthur was aware of disquieting developments. In the border states, during the summer, secret societies were being formed, with the avowed purpose of making Canada a republic. These societies were known as Hunters' Lodges, and the origin of the name is obscure. It appears to have been a translation of the name used by the *patriotes* of Lower Canada and their American allies who called their societies *Les frères chasseurs* and used Vermont as their headquarters. Both lodges were similar, with special signals and esoteric names for high-ranking officers.[12] Most Hunters' Lodges were formed in the United States, but a number appear to have been created in Upper and Lower Canada. Just how many existed in the two colonies is not known. The Hunters appear to have absorbed Henry Handy's western organization after its plans for a July attack on Windsor failed when a few brigands attacked Sarnia and caused security at the Detroit armoury, the expected source of weapons, to be increased.

That September a convention of lodges in Michigan and Ohio met at Cleveland, and formed a "Republican Government of Upper Canada". The commander-in-chief was Lucius V. Bierce, an attorney from Akron and a brigadier-general in the Ohio militia. Mackenzie, who, like many of the Canadian exiles, had withdrawn — or been excluded — from the movement he had started, was struggling to support his family in Rochester.[13] His active participation was for the most part at an end. The lodges enjoyed enormous support in the frontier states quickly building up a membership of tens of thousands, all of whom felt that Upper Canada was yearning for the kind of freedom that the U.S. had achieved with the Revolutionary War. Many of the politicians either belonged or gave support in the hope of obtaining votes. This widespread support made it relatively easy for the republicans to secure arms from state armouries and relatively difficult for the federal government to step in and stop any invasion of British territory, invasion which could cause a war with Britain.

Disturbed by reports of the Hunters' Lodges, Arthur sent the rest of the 34th Regiment to Amherstburg, and he received Colborne's permission to enlist Upper Canadians into regular regiments.[14] Apparently some men did, although such service could have had little appeal. Militia soldiers were often court martialled, and sentences ranged from dismissals to prison terms, but flogging was not permitted under the militia laws. The uniform could have been a lure, however. The militiamen were supposed to have red coatees faced blue, but few had received any by late 1838, while officers provided their own. Among the supplies sent to Kingston on 29 October were blue "Pilot Cloth", grey for trousers, and scarlet for facings.[15] The cloth may have been for the provincial artillery, whose uniforms were blue faced red, the same as those of the Royal Artillery.

Arthur's correspondence with Colborne reveals the tension that existed between the two. Writing to a friend on 20 September, Sir George was concerned about the vast distance that separated him from Quebec City. He was startled to learn that Sir John had told the Lords of Treasury that Arthur thought he had an independent command. Arthur maintained that although he knew he was in command of the forces in Upper Canada, he never doubted that he was Colborne's subordinate and subject to his orders.

To Colborne, Arthur explained that he felt duty bound to state his opinion, and that having to deal with Quebec City was inconvenient. An efficient commissariat was important to the militia, and with trouble brewing on his frontiers, more incorporated regiments would soon be required. If men were to turn out in a crisis, they had a right to expect to be well fed, clothed, quartered and armed. Arthur had been on tour as far as Cornwall, where he

Brockville in 1841 by Frederick H. Holloway. One traveller in the 1830s called Brockville "the prettiest town I saw in Upper Canada".

View of Fort George from Fort Niagara, New York, ca. 1812. The fort was badly damaged during the War of 1812.

Fort Mississauga at Niagara (Niagara-on-the-Lake).

found that many loyal people were disgruntled over the leniency shown rebel and invader alike. He now had six regiments of regulars, some 3,500 men, but most were stationed inland, in accordance with Colborne's wishes. Professionals would not be on hand if a blow should be struck without warning. [16]

When he replied, Colborne assured Arthur that a general officer at a distance from headquarters had the power to direct all operations in his district or province, as long as he reported directly to the commander-in-chief. Inevitably, their jurisdictions overlapped, since the shoreline east of Brockville was more accessible from Montreal than from Toronto. Colborne knew that Arthur was short of arms, but the delays in the delivery of weapons were occurring because shipments had not arrived from England. He referred to the confusion of "last winter" because of poor record-keeping. Headquarters could not pay claims where no proper receipts had been issued. Future claims would be honoured, because regular officers were meticulous about giving and keeping receipts.

Writing on 28 September, Colborne approved most of Arthur's suggestions for deploying the militia and regulars. A detachment of militia should be kept at Whitby, because of the disaffected people in the townships of Reach and Pickering. If any republicans should land at Baldwin's Creek, Duffin's Creek or the Rouge River, the sedentary militia should be embodied to assist regulars coming from Toronto. No regulars should be used where militia could cope. As long as a force of 1,200 regulars could be conveyed to a trouble spot in two or three days, an area that was menaced would not be left unprotected for long.

Whenever regulars were required to march from their forts and posts, these should be occupied by embodied militia. Gunboats should be kept near Sarnia, Sandwich and Port Dover, and on Lake Ontario at Whitby. A detachment of the 32nd Regiment, then at Simcoe, should return to London and be replaced by militia, and the barracks improved for the winter. All the troops must be kept comfortable to ensure their good health and spirits. The detachment of the 71st would be withdrawn from Brockville as soon as a company of pensioners could be formed under a half-pay officer. Colborne reminded Arthur that Lower Canada was in great danger, as a large quantity of arms had been smuggled into the Mississquoi Bay area. [17]

When Lord Durham resigned because he felt that the home government was not giving him enough support, Arthur made a trip to Quebec City to confer with him before he sailed for England.

Meanwhile Colborne ordered the Glengarry Militia to be ready to march to Lower Canada, noting that they were well supplied with arms. When Arthur returned he ordered a depot of 500 small arms for Prescott. He stopped at Belleville in response to a report of unrest from Captain George de Rottenburg, the unattached regular officer stationed there. As Arthur had often warned Colborne, "there is a very general disaffection in this Province in consequence it is asserted, of delay and ultimate injustice in settling the accounts after the last outbreak."[18]

Colborne had ordered more field pieces sent to Upper Canada, but Arthur was unhappy over so many referrals to headquarters, and his province was still ill-prepared. Full batteries at Kingston and Niagara, and a half-battery at London, were hardly sufficient artillery. The arms at many stations were unserviceable, and the ordnance department required that all be sent to Kingston for repairs. Having repairs carried out at the various stations would save time and transportation costs. The incorporated militiamen had turned in their arms upon discharge, but all needed cleaning and most required some work. Lieutenant-Colonel Henry Booth, at Niagara, had received 1,500 weapons, and he did not want them moved to Kingston. If Colborne agreed, Booth's regimental armourer would fix them. Arthur wanted as much work as possible done on the spot,

Butler's Barracks at Niagara (Niagara-on-the-Lake). The original Butler's Barracks was destroyed during the War of 1812. A second barracks complex was begun following the War and used for troops during 1837.

for delays would give invading republicans a temporary advantage.

In the northern states meanwhile the Hunters were making prepartions for an assault on Upper Canada on 1 November, co-ordinated with an invasion of Lower Canada by *Les frères chasseurs*. The secret plans were not very secret and in October, Arthur was receiving and transmitting to Colborne very specific rumours. On 22 October Arthur wrote to Lord Glenelg reporting the conspiracy and detailing his response. An officer was being sent to the Niagara frontier to spy on the Hunters; a messenger was being sent to the British minister in Washington asking him to press the American government for action. Another officer was being sent to ask the assistance of General Macomb, the commander of the American regulars on the border. In addition, at the urging of the executive council, Arthur was calling out part of the sedentary militia. This latter action was carried out on the 23rd.[19]

There was always some question as to how far Arthur could go in reacting to a perceived threat without Colborne's permission, but in this case, Colborne shared the same worry. Writing on 21

The military hospital at Niagara as it looked in 1864. This house, or others like it, would have been used as hospitals in the 1830s.

October, Colborne warned Arthur that the situation was grave. Henry Stephen Fox, the British ambassador in Washington, had notified him that an:

> alarming organization exists in the States of Vermont, New York, Ohio, Illinois and Michigan, and that the Collectors at the different Ports all concur in their reports as to the extent of the sympathising societies, and of the preparations for invasion. [20]

In response to this threat Colborne wrote on the 21st that he was raising volunteer corps for permanent duty, the sedentary militia to be held in reserve, and he ordered Arthur to do the same. If he found that men were unwilling to enlist, he was to raise corps on such terms as he thought necessary. Privates could be allowed ten shillings per month of service upon discharge. Where they had been given two pounds on enlistment they only wasted this money on liquor. Colborne wanted the incorporated battalions and companies considered provincial regulars, since permitting militia law to apply would restrict the way the men could be used.

He asked Arthur to allow Colonel Alexander Fraser of the 1st Glengarry Regiment and Colonel Donald Macdonell (Greenfield) of the 2nd, to embody 600 men each for permanent duty in Lower Canada. The men would be paid two shillings and sixpence currency a day while on active service. Colonel Philip VanKoughnett was to embody 400 of his 2nd Stormont Regiment at Cornwall. Many independent companies needed to be raised along the vulnerable parts of the frontier, and Major Thomas Magrath must call out his Lancers to keep order along Yonge Street. [21] Arthur had responded by issuing Militia General Orders for the enlistment of four incorporated battalions/regiments, and twelve provisional battalions as a reserve force. All sixteen battalions would be commanded by lieutenant-colonels. Unlike their predecessors, the new incorporated regiments were never named, and were identified only by their numbers. The incorporated battalions were to serve for eighteen months, the provisional for six.

Incorporated	Commander	Headquarters
1st	Sir Allan MacNab	Hamilton
2nd	Kenneth Cameron	London
3rd	William Kingsmill	Toronto
4th	Joseph Hill	Kingston

Provisional	Commander	Headquarters
1st	Peter Adamson	Port Credit
2nd	Amos Thorne	Toronto
3rd	Philip VanKoughnett	Cornwall
4th	Donald Macdonell	Charlottenburgh Township
5th	Alexander Fraser	Lancaster Township
6th	Connell J. Baldwin	Toronto
7th	Alexander Macdonell	Peterborough
8th	Allen Macdonell	Kingston
9th	Ogle Gowan	Brockville
10th	James Kerby	Fort Erie
11th	Thomas Radcliffe	Adelaide Township
12th	Alexander McMillan	Perth

The two Black companies serving under Major Richard Webbe on the Niagara frontier would be increased to eighty men each. Major Webbe was to select new officers to command them. Captain James Sears was not a capable leader, while Captain Thomas Runchey had had to resign in July. Afterwards Runchey absconded to the United States leaving his accounts in disarray. Lieutenant-Colonel Booth held a court martial on 8 August which found the absent Runchey an unfit officer, for funds he had drawn had not been used to pay his men. Two Black companies, to be raised at Chatham, would be commanded by Captains George Muttlebury and James Black Perrier. Twenty-eight other independent companies were to be raised across the province. A Militia General Order announced that some 9000 volunteers were needed to serve in independent volunteer companies to be stationed at sensitive spots along the frontier and around the capital. Over the next weeks these companies were gradually created. [22]

Colborne knew he could not expect much help from the United States, other than the good will of the army officers. General Alexander Macomb, the American commander-in-chief on the northern frontier, was willing to keep Colborne informed on the strength of his various stations. He allowed a British regular officer, Lieutenant Thomas William Jones, to visit his posts. On 30 October Jones reported that Macomb had 2,000 United States regulars stationed from Troy, Vermont, to Fort Gratiot, at the entrance to the St. Clair River. The American posts bordering Upper Canada were at French Mills, southwest of Cornwall; at Sackets Harbor, across

Lake Ontario from Kingston where Colonel William Worth commanded; at Fort Niagara, opposite the town of Niagara; at Buffalo where Macomb had his headquarters; and at Detroit where General Hugh Brady commanded. Arthur knew that so few regulars could do little to control the thousands of restless republicans, yet he did not object to sending some of his militia to serve under Colborne. [23]

The 4th and 5th Provisional Battalions, from Glengarry, left Cornwall, and on 10 November a disturbance broke out at Beauharnois. This proved to be the start of a second large-scale rebellion in Lower Canada. Once he saw how serious the situation had become, Colborne ordered Major Lewis Carmichael, then at Cornwall, to assemble more reinforcements at once. Carmichael was to move them along the south shore of the St. Lawrence to avoid Beauharnois. The major embodied 889 rank and file from the remains of the four Glengarry regiments, the Cornwall Volunteer Cavalry, the Brockville Volunteer Artillery, the detachment of the 71st Regiment that had been in Brockville, and twenty-one Royal Sappers and Miners under Major Phillpotts. [24]

On Sunday 11 November, the day on which Major Carmichael received Colborne's order to go to Lower Canada, some 400 republicans left Sackets Harbor and other ports of call aboard the steamer *United States* bound for Prescott. What followed was the most controversial of all the border raids. Even men who fought on the same side reported different versions of what happened and differing statistics on the numbers killed, wounded or captured.

Chapter 11

Battle of the Windmill, 11-16 November 1838

S urprising, in retrospect, is the tenacity with which members of the Hunters' Lodges clung to the belief that Canadians longed for their own independence movement. Whenever a force of republicans landed, despite setbacks, they still expected to be greeted by thousands of eager freedom fighters who had been marking time until their American brethren could arrive to liberate them. Another serious outrage occurred in November of 1838. The preparations by the authorities in Upper Canada to repel invasion convinced the Hunter leadership to call off their part of the co-ordinated attack on the two Canadas, as had been planned for November, even though the *Chasseurs* went ahead with their invasion of Lower Canada. It was often true, though, that one part of the Hunter organization or another insisted on local direction of its affairs. "General" John Ward Birge, the Hunter commander for the eastern section of the American frontier, continued plans for a November invasion. Birge, who was from Cazenovia, New York, believed that a surprise invasion could still be made. The objective would be Prescott and Fort Wellington. This spot was close to the American shore, sat right on the main line of communication to Lower Canada, and was as good as any place to cause a rising by the oppressed Canadians.

Among the prominent men on the frontier who assisted in organizing the Hunters were "Colonel" Martin Woodruff of Salina, sheriff of Onondaga County and a colonel in the New York militia, and Dorephus Abbey, a newspaper editor, from Pamelia in Jefferson County. Both were to figure prominently in the attack on Upper Canada. The man who would ultimately be in charge of one of the most serious of the border raids was Nils von Schoultz of Salina, New York, a romantic figure who had deliberately thrown a smoke screen over his past life.

Von Schoultz, when the raid brought him to prominence, was a hero to Americans, and he also found much sympathy among Canadians, but the story he told was a web of fact and fiction. He claimed to be an exile from Poland, who as an officer in the Polish army had fought the Russians. He had seen his father, a regimental

Nils von Schoultz, the handsome, personable cad who commanded the invaders at the windmill. He claimed to be a Polish exile, but in reality he was a Swedish national.

commander, killed in action, his mother and sister sent into exile in Siberia. He viewed the oppressed Canadians as suffering the same fate as the peasants of Poland, and he resolved to help them throw off the cruel and tyrannical British yoke of slavery. He was a devout Roman Catholic who had left a fiancée in Syracuse.

The truth was that he was Finnish-born and a Swedish national, who for a short time held a commission in the Polish army during the Polish struggle for independence. He did escape from the Russians in 1831 after being taken prisoner, but then he joined the French Foreign Legion. After less than a year he left the Legion in 1832, and soon married a Scottish woman, while visiting Florence, Italy. In England, unable to support his wife and two young children, he boarded a ship for New York to seek his fortune in America. Later posing as a qualified chemist, he found a job in a salt manufacturing plant in Salina.[1] He soon joined the local Hunters Lodge, swayed by fellow members' accounts of the poor downtrodden Canadians, who resembled the poor people of Poland.

Nils left with other members of his lodge for Sackets Harbor, the main rallying point for invading Hunters, although members of some lodges were gathering at other points along the New York shore. Beforehand, some republicans had seized two Lake Ontario schooners, the *Charlotte of Oswego* and the *Charlotte of Toronto*. On the morning of Sunday 11 November, the American steamer *United States*, with Captain James Van Cleve in command, was downbound for Ogdensburg when she stopped at Sackets Harbor. The town had been filled to overflowing the previous week, but when the *United States* was delayed for some days it was decided to disperse the men to other stops along the steamer's route. It appears that when this decision was taken, a substantial number of men chose to go home instead. Perhaps a hundred men had already boarded at Oswego and at this stop some 70-80 men went on board, while others joined the steamer at Cape Vincent, Clayton, French Creek, and Millen's Bay, all regular stops.

Off Millen's Bay, Van Cleve agreed to take in tow the two schooners, containing some 200 men, the republicans remaining below out of sight. Van Cleve was not surprised at the request for the tow, for the breeze was light and he had often aided sailing vessels in the past. After the schooners had been made fast to the sides of the steamer, the Hunters emerged, over 400 including those on the steamer, clad in a bewildering array of home-made uniforms, no two alike. Bill Johnston, who had joined the steamer at Clayton, sported a red officer's sash and a "Cochran rifle, two large rifle pistols, and tucked into his waistband, several pistols and a foot long Bowie knife". For the tow and the fares of the Hunters on the *United States*, Captain Van Cleve was paid $100. This did not mean that he supported what the Hunters were doing. His conduct at Morristown showed quite the opposite.[2]

The American steamer *United States* which brought many of the republicans (self-styled patriots) to Ogdensburg. The drawing is by C.H.J. Snider and was probably based on a pen and ink sketch by an earlier artist.

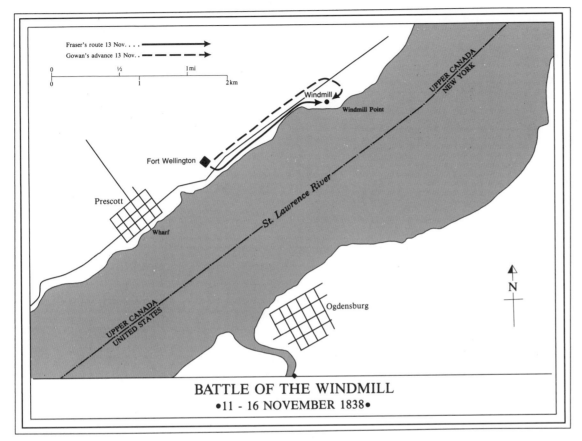

BATTLE OF THE WINDMILL
•11 - 16 NOVEMBER 1838•

Map labels: Fraser's route 13 Nov...., Gowan's advance 13 Nov.., Windmill, Windmill Point, UPPER CANADA / NEW YORK, Fort Wellington, Prescott, Wharf, St. Lawrence River, UPPER CANADA / UNITED STATES, Ogdensburg, N

Colonel William Worth, the American federal commander on the New York frontier. Worth was already out searching for the republican craft which were well ahead of him. At Brockville the small armed steamer *Experiment* was patrolling the river in front of the town, where it was felt an attack was likely.[3]

As the *United States* left Morristown and crossed the river, it resumed towing the two schooners full of men. In the dark, the steamer came up on the *Experiment*, patrolling off Brockville, and quickly retreated to the American side of the river. Luckily the two schooners were not seen and no alarm was raised. Not long afterwards the two schooners were released. Birge stayed on the *United States* to Ogdensburg to get reinforcements from among the many Hunters in the port, while the men on the two schooners made course for the dock at Prescott hoping to make a surprise attack on the town and Fort Wellington beyond. The schooners were either lashed together as they crossed or they became entangled during the crossing, so that when they arrived at the town it was very difficult to manoeuvre into the dock The time was about 2:00 a.m. on 12 November.

As the *United States* approached Morristown, most of the republicans transferred to the schooners. Bill Johnston, in his capacity as admiral of their navy, took command of the *Charlotte of Oswego*. The two schooners were cut loose while the *United States* made its scheduled stop. Before resuming his downward way Van Cleve, in co-operation with a few passengers, alerted the local magistrate and asked him to inform the U.S marshall at Ogdesnburg, or the magistrate there. On the Canadian side, rumours of a Hunter invasion had kept the populace on edge for several days. Earlier that day word had reached Captain Williams Sandom, the British naval commander at Kingston, that two schooners were waiting at Sackets Harbor for a tow from the *United States* in order to attack Toronto or some place on the St. Lawrence. Sandom had sailed with the armed steamers *Cobourg* and *Queen Victoria* to the American side to warn

The garrison at Prescott and in the fort consisted of over 100 embodied Grenville militia and volunteers from Prescott, together with 35 Glengarries under Captain George Macdonell of Lancaster Township. All were commanded by Major Plomer Young, an unattached regular officer who held the local rank of lieutenant-colonel. A guard had been mounted at the wharf because of the strong rumours of attack and more men were awake in the town. Those on sentry duty on the dock hailed the schooners, which were vainly trying to dock quickly. The Hunters on the schooners realized that they could not make a surprise landing and put out into the St. Lawrence. Some of the men on the schooners later claimed that a sentry also fired on them. As they went out, the craft separated and sailed independently. In the dark the *Oswego* grounded on the muddy delta of the Oswegatchie River. The *Toronto* anchored nearby while a decision was made as to the next move.[4]

While the militia at Prescott was being roused, word was sent to Brockville asking for help. When he received the news, Lieutenant-Colonel Ogle Gowan, the commander of the fledgling 9th Provisional Battalion (Queen's Royal Borderers), set about organizing his men. The embodied Leeds militia could protect Brockville while Gowan led two companies of his battalion to the aid of the militia at Prescott. During the morning he dispatched messengers to Colonel William Marshall, the regular officer at Gananoque, to Lieutenant-Colonel Henry Dundas of the 83rd Regiment at Kingston, to the militia officers in the back townships of the Johnstown District and to those of the Bathurst District, asking them to come to Gananoque, Brockville, and Prescott. Well before dawn, the *Experiment* steamed down river to guard the water approach to Prescott.[5]

With daylight, the *United States*, carrying Birge, came out of Ogdensburg to meet with the Hunters in the schooners. After some discussion it was decided that the *Toronto* would land her men at Windmill Point, about a mile further down the river. Meanwhile the *United States* would free the *Oswego* so that the men and supplies in her could be landed. The *Toronto* headed for the point while the *United States* passed a line to the larger schooner. Lieutenant William Fowell, who commanded the *Experiment*, thought that the *United States* was sailing towards Prescott and he moved to the attack. The American steamboat was much larger than the British one which carried only a crew of 25, but the *Experiment's* armament was formidable. She carried an 18-pounder carronade and a 3-pounder brass field piece. Fowell opened fire with the carronade and the *United States* retreated to the American side.

The *Experiment* could not pursue the *Toronto* since the defence of Prescott against attack by water was Fowell's chief concern. The men on the schooner were thus able to get ashore with ease.[6]

Windmill Point was an ideal spot to use as a base. Surrounding the windmill was the tiny hamlet of New Jerusalem, whose stone houses could be used for cover. The walls of the six-storey windmill were thick and snipers could be posted at openings near the top.

Since Birge and Johnston were not with them, the men at the windmill decided to elect their own leader, choosing von Schoultz, a popular figure with a military background. He in turn chose to have both Woodruff and Abbey as seconds-in-command. A party was quickly sent out to block the road from Brockville. It partially succeeded in destroying the bridge at Honeywell's Bay, a mile west of the town, and it captured two militia dragoons. The remainder of the men occupied New Jerusalem and hoisted the "patriot" flag from the top of the windmill. This was a blue silk banner emblazoned with the words "Liberated by the Onondaga Hunters" which had been presented to von Schoultz in Salina.[7]

The Hunters at Ogdensburg were determined to land more men at the windmill.

The British steamer *Experiment* that was dispatched from Brockville to prevent any more "patriots" crossing the St. Lawrence.

When the *United States* could not free the *Oswego* during a second attempt, small boats and the *Toronto*, which had returned to the U.S. side, were used to remove some of the men and three small cannon from the *Oswego* and to carry them to the Canadian shore. Towards noon the steam ferry *Paul Pry*, which usually operated between Ogdensburg and Prescott, was commandeered and brought out to tow the *Oswego*. Having a shallow draft, the ferry could move in closer to the grounded schooner. When the *Paul Pry* came out, Fowell again attacked, thinking the two American boats were heading for Prescott. Although the men on the ferry and the schooner kept up a heavy musket fire, the *Experiment* forced the *Paul Pry* to retreat and the schooner to surrender. Only another sortie by the *United States* saved the men of the *Oswego* from a British prison.

While the schooner slipped back to the American side, the *Experiment* turned her muskets and carronade on the *United States*, driving it back and beheading the helmsman. General Birge who was on board the American steamer became very "ill" during this action and was not to be seen again until the invasion was over. Having cleared the river in front of Prescott, the *Experiment*, which was having trouble with its main armament, retreated to protect the town and the republicans were able to transport men and materials to Windmill Point for the rest of the day. Unfortunately for von Schoultz and his men, no one thought to bring over the proper sized balls for the Hunter cannon.[8]

It is impossible to tell how many men went to join von Schoultz and his party. Even Bill Johnston spent a short time visiting the Canadian shore, promising to return the next day with reinforcements. When the last boat left the point Monday night, a substantial number of the men who were there, including some of those who had come in the *Toronto*, returned to the American side. Probably slightly over 200 remained. This figure seems about right given that the British later captured about 160 and estimated that about thirty had died. The remainder slipped away during the days of siege that followed. Of the republicans, 29 were "British subjects", from the two Canadas and the British Isles. Bill Johnston tried to get more men to go across from Ogdensburg but his appeal fell on deaf ears.

Von Schoultz and his men settled in to wait for the oppressed Canadians and their fellow Hunters to join them, but this was not to be the case. Few of the hundreds of Hunters and Hunter supporters around Ogdensburg now wanted to join their fellows. The British soon made the river crossing very dangerous and, on the Canadian side, there was far more anger at the invasion than support for it. Judge Levius Sherwood, for instance, described the invaders as "a band of foreign Marauders and fugitive traitors that lately joined in a conspiracy against the Constitution and Government of the Country, and landed and took up a hostile position at Prescott".[9]

Ogle Gowan left Brockville with his two companies (150 men) early in the morning and they stopped to repair the bridge which von Schoultz's men had demolished at Honeywell's Bay, before they continued to Prescott. In the afternoon Gowan's men joined those twenty or so of the Grenville militia who were posted near the windmill. Young had chosen to keep most of his men in Prescott to defend the town until he could attack. More reinforcements were on the way. Captain George Markley arrived with some 200 Stormont and Dundas militia while, around dusk, 120-150 men from Glengarry joined what was becoming a thickening circle of opponents surrounding the windmill and the buildings of New Jerusalem. Around 2.00 a.m. on Tuesday the 13th, the two armed steamers *Queen Victoria* and *Cobourg* had arrived from Kingston under the command of Captain Williams Sandom. Aboard the steamers were forty-four regulars from the 83rd Regiment and thirty Royal Marines.

The American federal authorities were also determined to stop the invasion. Nathaniel Garrow, a United States marshal, and Colonel William Worth were following the Hunters to Ogdensburg with two companies of American regulars. No more republicans were to be allowed to cross the river. The two officers arrived on the night of the 12th, and Garrow seized the *Charlotte of Oswego* and the steamers *United States* and *Paul Pry* for violations of the Neutrality Act. Captain Van Cleve objected, stating that his ship had been commandeered, which was probably true. The marshal chose to believe the republicans who had remained in Ogdensburg, who claimed that Van Cleve had been paid and was a willing party to the scheme.

At the windmill a drizzling rain was falling, and the assembled militiamen and regulars spent a miserable night. Very early on the morning of the 13th, Lieutenant-Colonel Plomer Young resolved to take action, partly because he felt that the men could not remain in such an uncomfortable situation much longer. He ordered a dawn attack on the republicans' position in two columns, the right one to be led by Lieutenant-Colonel Ogle Gowan, the left by Lieutenant-Colonel Richard Duncan Fraser of the 2nd Grenville Regiment.

The Battle of the Windmill as seen from Ogdensburg. This engraving was taken from Charles Lindsey's biography of Mackenzie.

Gowan's vanguard was led by Lieutenant William Johnson of the 83rd Regiment, who had forty-four of his regulars with him. Fraser's vanguard consisted of thirty Royal Marines led by Lieutenant Charles Parker. Gowan's column advanced from Fort Wellington along the shore, while Fraser's swung inland to approach the windmill from the northeast. Probably 475 to 500 men took part. By the time the men marched, Lieutenant Fowell, aboard the *Experiment*, was directing the shelling from all three steamers against the windmill.

Inside, von Schoultz watched as the columns formed battle lines and, to his dismay, what he had hoped were reinforcements coming to his flag was an attacking force. He sent his men out into the field beyond the buildings in open order, telling them to hold their fire until he gave the word. Excited at the prospect of action, the invaders ignored their chosen leader, and began firing almost at once. The British and Canadian left, composed of the men of the Marines and Glengarries, made slow progress against this strong fire but Gowan's vanguard meanwhile flanked the enemy on the right, coming under accurate fire from the men left in the mill in the process. Then the left also managed to flank the invaders. With their flanks turned, the republicans were forced to retreat to the buildings, but once there they were well protected. Cannon balls from the *Queen Victoria* and the *Cobourg* were more threatening to the militia and the regulars than to the republicans. The windmill stood on a bluff above the river, and the gunners had to aim high.

After the first assault, Lieutenant-Colonel Young called off further attempts, to avoid even heavier casualties. He noted that the cannon balls from the *Queen Victoria* and the *Cobourg* which struck the windmill were bouncing off the thick walls. After the regulars and militiamen withdrew out of range of von Schoultz's sharpshooters stationed in the upper openings of the windmill, Young sent a request to Kingston for reinforcements of regulars and artillery. Parties of regulars and militia harrassed the Hunters for the rest of the day and the *Cobourg* and the *Experiment* were on patrol in the river to prevent further crossings. A few small boats did get across, though, and a few of the invaders escaped.[10]

Under a flag of truce, on Wednesday morning the 14th, both sides sent men into the battlefield to take out the dead and wounded. Lieutenant William Johnson of the 83rd Regiment, and Lieutenant John Dulmage, a son of Lieutenant-Colonel Philip Dulmage of the 1st Grenville Regiment, had been killed. One other regular was killed, and nineteen regulars were wounded. Militia casualties were one other officer and twelve rank and file killed, and three officers and forty-five rank and file wounded. Hunter losses were perhaps thirteen dead and twenty-eight wounded, but the records are conflicting. They had not brought any medical supplies. Since theirs was to have been a bloodless victory, they had not burdened themselves with such excess baggage. The body of Lieutenant Johnson was reported to have been mutilated, and when on 14

The British steamer *Traveller* which plied Lake Ontario and the St. Lawrence from 1835 to 1866. The drawing is by C.H.J. Snider.

109

November the Canadians learned of this breach of the rules of war, their indignation knew no bounds. The force encircling von Schoultz's position by Tuesday night had grown by several hundred men. According to Lieutenant-Colonel Young's report, the militia detachments present by the end of the battle were elements of the Queen's Royal Borderers, the Glengarries, the Stormont, Dundas and Grenville regiments, the Brockville independent company, under Captain Robert Edmondson, Captain Hamilton D. Jessup's independent company from Prescott, a number of gentleman volunteers, and some Grenville cavalry. Companies of men continued to arrive all day from more distant areas. Gowan's men was then sent home since it had done its duty in the battle and there was a sufficient militia force to replace it.

The citizens of Ogdensburg had a ringside seat and were very excited. This excitement did not lead to aid for von Schoultz, however, even from those who wished to cross to Upper Canada, for now Marshal Garrow and Colonel Worth's soldiers were stopping most of their attempts to communicate with the men in the windmill. Throughout Wednesday von Schoultz watched for reinforcements from Ogdensburg that would never come. His situation was worsening, because of the desertions on Monday and Tuesday. That night a man named Meredith paddled across the icy water on a plank with news of the desperate position of the republicans, who had no balls for their cannon and were surrounded. Meredith also reported on the plight of the wounded, lying untended in the windmill. Birge suggested that Bill Johnston create a diversion by attacking Gananoque.

Late Tuesday night, Lieutenant-Colonel Henry Dundas had arrived from Kingston with four fresh companies of his 83rd Regiment, Major Forbes Macbean of the Royal Artillery and two field pieces. After surveying the situation, Macbean and Dundas returned to Kingston to arrange to bring heavier artillery, taking with them the regulars and marines who had fought on Tuesday. As the *Cobourg* and *Queen Victoria* were needed to bring up more men it was possible for one or two small boats to avoid the *Experiment* and another armed vessel and slip across the Canadian side to take off a few of the Hunters. One boat reputedly carried Bill Johnston, who announced that he would be back that night to rescue the remaining Hunters. A large number of small boats were prepared to come across but the British patrol discouraged them, and no rescue took place.[11]

On Thursday the 15th, Colonel Worth and Captain Sandom met with Lieutenant-Colonel Young aboard the American steamer *Telegraph* under a flag of truce. Worth asked Young to allow the republicans inside the windmill to go to the American side in return for prosecution of the invaders in the United States and guarantee that the United States Army would prevent further invasions, but Young refused. Perhaps he felt he could not act without Sir George Arthur's approval, or he was as angry as his men over the whole

Captain (left) and private (right) in the 93rd Regiment. The grenadier company was sent to Prescott in November 1838. The rest of the regiment moved to Upper Canada that December.

situation. Worth promised to seal the river against further attacks.

That night, with the *Experiment* out of action until 2.00 a.m., the steamer *Paul Pry* slipped out of Ogdensburg harbour under the noses of Worth's men, carrying a party of men, among them Preston King, the postmaster, who had some influence over the local people. King came to persuade von Schoultz to evacuate the windmill, but one of the men who had come on the *Paul Pry* jumped out first and announced that reinforcements would be coming. When King followed, the men on shore were confused as to what to do. The ferry then let off steam as it waited and warned the British forces. The *Paul Pry* quickly left with a few wounded and the last

opportunity for escape was lost.[12]

On Friday,16 November, Lieutenant-Colonel Henry Dundas and Major Forbes Macbean returned from Kingston bringing four more companies of the 83rd and two 18-pounder guns and a howitzer. When Sir John Colborne was notified of events near Prescott, he sent the grenadier company of the 93rd Regiment, commanded by Major John Arthur, that had been at Beauharnois quelling rebels there, and some more Glengarries, to join the reinforcement of regulars from Kingston.[13] That morning, Colonel Fraser had a meeting with von Schoultz to arrange to pick up the dead. Von Schoultz offered him the British wounded as well since the

View of Prescott and the windmill in 1876. By that time the windmill had been converted to a lighthouse.

republicans had no medical supplies. About 1:00 p.m. Dundas arrived with the extra troops and the heavy artillery. At 3:00 p.m., just as the battle commenced, the men of the 93rd arrived.

Major MacBean ordered one of his 18-pounders placed in front of the windmill, and the howitzer and the other 18-pounder on the left. These opened fire, as did the two gunboats and at least one armed steamer. The Hunters returned the fire sporadically with cannon loaded with hinges, bolts, and other bits of metal, and the odd 6-pound ball fired by the British field pieces and picked up by the besieged republicans. Soon the stone buildings around the mill were reduced to piles of rubble, which were set on fire by the advancing troops. The mill's defenders were safe even from the heavy artillery but were gradually worn down to the point where they decided to surrender. Woodruff ordered a white flag flown from the top of the mill, but even after it was in place the firing continued. A small party of men volunteered to carry a flag towards the British lines, but they were immediately fired on and had to run for cover. Then about 6:00 p.m. in consultation with Sandom, Dundas ordered a temporary ceasefire in order to call upon the invaders to surrender. Sandom later reported, as justification for stopping the attack that it was growing dark, but he is reputed to have been angry that the British forces were firing on a white flag.

When the British forces showed a white flag, Martin Woodruff quickly led his exhausted men out of the mill. As the Hunters filed out, infuriated militiamen began to abuse the prisoners, and Dundas had to order his regulars to protect them. The victors looked among the prisoners for von Schoultz, but he was nowhere to be found. When the battle commenced, he and some other men had taken positions in a house near the mill. The house had been destroyed in the fighting and von Schoultz was forced to retreat. Later, Eustace Fell and Edward Smith of the Prescott Independent Company found the unhappy Swede hiding in some bushes near the river and marched him off to Prescott where the other prisoners had been taken. Some 131 Hunters and Canadian rebels were put aboard the steamer *Cobourg* for transport to Kingston, after a march through lines of hostile Prescott citizens.

At Kingston the prisoners were roped together by their necks in a long line with von Schoultz in the lead. Again they moved between lines of angry faces, protected by the regulars, the band of the 83rd Regiment playing "Yankee Doodle". At Fort Henry they were confined in large barrack rooms, and thirty-nine who were under twenty-one were segregated from the rest. Two lawyers from Ogdensburg — John Fine and Charles Myers — visited the young lads. After they left Kingston the lawyers sent a request to Sir George Arthur for the release of the under-age prisoners. Arthur conferred with Judge Jonas Jones, and he decided that they would ultimately be released, but not before they had been tried by court martial, scheduled to begin on 28 November. [14]

Of the many funerals that followed, Lieutenant William Johnson's attracted the most attention. The cortege started from the Tete de Pont barracks. In the lead was the party that would fire the salute at the graveside. The band of the 83rd Regiment followed, and after it the leading citizens of Kingston. Behind them marched the men of the 83rd with black crepe on their shakos, followed by other officers and men of the Royal Navy and the militia units. Afterwards a cannon and a detachment of militia were stationed at the windmill where Johnson fell, to ensure that the building would not be used a second time by invaders. [15]

When word of the landing near Prescott reached the Bathurst District, a battle of quite another stripe broke out. Sir Francis Head had appointed, as the lieutenant-colonel of the 2nd Carleton Regiment, Archibald McNab, the seventeenth chief of clan MacNab (or McNab). The chief had brought some clansmen to Upper Canada, and was granted the Township of McNab, where he proceeded to dictate to his people to the point where they felt severely oppressed. They had sent a message to Lieutenant Governor Head affirming their loyalty, but stating that they had suffered enough at the hands of their chief under civil law. They were appalled at the thought of serving under him when he could use military law to bully them.

On 16 November McNab called out his regiment, which was drawn from the townships of McNab, Fitzroy and Pakenham. The men mustered at Pakenham village, where McNab called for volunteers. Those from Fitzroy and Pakenham, for the most part Irish, responded willingly. Those from McNab held back. The Irish from Fitzroy and Pakenham called them poltroons, and a pitched battle began. Outnumbered five to one, the McNab settlers retreated to the house of a Mrs. McFarlane, and defended themselves with frying pans, pokers, tongs, kettles, brooms and anything else that came to hand. The fight went on all night, until everyone was exhausted. Many had nasty wounds, and one man named Porter died ten days later. By that time word had reached the townships of the defeat of von Schoultz's force, and the militia would not be needed [16]

While the affair at Windmill Point was holding the attention of the people in the easterly districts, tensions continued along other sensitive parts of the frontier. Rumours spread that attacks were planned for the Windsor-Sandwich-Amherstburg area, and along the Niagara River. On 16 November, the day von Schoultz's followers surrendered, Captain Edgeworth Ussher, of Lieutenant-Colonel Kerby's 10th Provisional Battalion, was assassinated at Chippawa. He was gunned down at the door of his house, and the man believed responsible was Benjamin Lett. [17]

Bill Johnston was caught in the woods near Ogdensburg a few days later by two local men and conveyed to Sackets Harbor. From there he was moved south to Auburn and placed in a hotel under guard. Also there and under arrest was "General" Birge, the coward who had left his expedition at Ogdensburg pleading illness. Both men escaped, and Johnston was soon caught near Rome, New York, and taken to Albany for trial. He was sentenced to one year in jail and fined $250, and his daughter Kate came from Clayton to share his incarceration. [18]

Chapter 12
Windsor and Other Alarms

On 14 November, in the middle of the Prescott crisis, Arthur wrote to Lord Glenelg explaining that although Colborne had authorized the calling out of the sedentary militia to deal with the expected attack on Upper Canada, the men were turning out very slowly. While he believed that they would come forward if there was an invasion, he was concerned that they would not turn out in advance, to prevent such an occurrence. When even the action at the windmill did not seem to be making any difference in enrollment, he became quite pessimistic about filling the quota voluntarily.[1]

For many reasons the militiamen were reluctant to accept permanent duty. Some felt that one month's service was all they could spare from their civilian lives. Others were affronted that they had had to wait a long time before they were paid, and certain of the officers had been harsh and inefficient. The men of the 5th Middlesex Regiment, from the townships of Caradoc, Ekfred and Mosa, complained about their colonel, James Craig, to Adjutant-General of Militia Richard Bullock. The regiment had been stationed on the Detroit frontier earlier in 1838, and Craig had failed to procure mattresses. The men had slept on bare boards in their clothes with vermin about, and Craig had kept them on duty after he was supposed to discharge them. When he finally did so, they were given neither pay nor provisions to sustain them on the journey back to their homes. Craig was also suspected of having exchanged part of £100 drawn from the commissary for his men, for Michigan bank

notes for his personal use.

In November Colonel John Prince, from Sandwich, told Arthur that the slow rate of enlistment was due to anger against the commissariat, while Lieutenant-Colonel Airey of the 34th, writing from Amherstburg, blamed much of the problem on the fact that the men had not been paid for earlier service, and that claims against the commissariat were regularly cut down before they were paid. While

A blockhouse that was built to protect one of the approaches to Toronto. John Ross Robertson identified it as standing on Sherbourne Street. Another source suggests the east side of Yonge Street opposite Belmont Street.

H.M.S. *Cherokee* lying off Kingston. In the background is Admiralty House, during the rebellion era the residence of Captain William Fowell, Royal Navy.

shuddering over the Battle of the Windmill. The 73rd, like the 71st, was a Highland regiment, but it did not look the part. Uniform in 1838 was the same as for the other regiments of the line. [3]

Ideally, Arthur would have liked to place more regular troops close to the border to deal with any invasion. After the next invasion, he was to write, regarding the western frontier:

> It is very well to talk of our Gallant Militia, but they are just what may be expected of officers and men totally untrained. If they ever meet with a reverse before they get into better order, it will be most injurious, and therefore in spite of all its disadvantages, some arrangement appears to be essential to give them some Detachment of regular Troops to form upon and be instructed by.[4]

Arthur was reluctant to blame the commissariat he realized that one demand, for blankets, had to be met, or the men would not turn out for winter service. He authorized the discreet purchase of blankets in the U.S., if necessary.

Bullock received complaints that some units had been used frequently, while others had never been embodied. The 1st Gore Regiment, of Brantford Township, had been called out repeatedly, while the 4th Gore, of Dumfries, had never been called out at all. This happened because the men of Dumfries had been considered untrustworthy. [2] With enlistment going slowly, Arthur issued a Militia General Order on 19 November for a draft to bring his force to 12,000 citizen-soldiers, an unpopular move, but the military situation seemed critical. He deployed detachments along the frontiers, with extra companies on the Welland Canal and had blockhouses built on the approaches to Toronto.

Sir John Colborne dispatched the 73rd Regiment of Foot to Upper Canada at the end of November. The commander was Lieutenant-Colonel Frederick Love, a Waterloo veteran. He led his men on to Brantford, except for a subaltern (Ensign, and later Lieutenant) William Hervey FitzGerald and thirty rank and file that Colborne ordered left in Brockville. People there were still

In early December, however, he was very reluctant to place regulars so close to the United States because of the desertion problem. Instead, he left it to the militia on most parts of the border to be the first line of defence.

On that border, a series of small incursions and rumours of a major invasion had kept nerves on edge all summer and fall. Rumours were very strong in November of an attack to be made on 21 November. The American general Hugh Brady had seized a schooner loaded with arms, and stories circulated of hundreds of republicans gathering on the American side of the St. Clair river. When the invasion, which was actually planned, did not take place, Arthur apparently felt that he now had enough men under arms to deal with any limited incursion. On 1 December he ordered an end to further recruiting, enlisting and enrollment, and drafting of militia for active service. By this time, the adjutant general calculated that he had 20,000 men under arms. Arthur later stated that he called out 13,000 militia in November alone. On the western frontier, however, the militia force on active service was still under strength.[5]

On 3 December another group of republicans was poised to enter the province, near Windsor, then a tiny village. Close by was the farm of François Baby, whose family had been in the neighbourhood since the 1700s. Baby was a former member of the legislature for Essex County. Sergeant Frederick Walsh and twenty-eight men of the 2nd Essex were quartered in a barracks near the Detroit River, while some militiamen under Lieutenant-Colonel John

John Prince ca. 1830. This miniature of Prince is the property of a descendant, John H. Prince.

Watercolour of John Prince ca. 1860. That year, Prince was appointed Judge of the district of Algoma.

Prince were three miles downriver at Sandwich.

On the evening of 3 December, in Detroit, "General" Lucius V. Bierce with probably 250 to 300 men took over the American steamer *Champlain* that was plying the Detroit River. Bierce had done everything he could to avoid coming over, to the point where much of his original force had given up in disgust, but was shamed into bringing the remainder. At 2.00 a.m. on the 4th they landed at a farm some three miles above Windsor. According to one version, the steamer left so that no one could desert, and the men marched to the village. Sergeant Walsh's men resisted the attackers until they were out of ammunition, then they attempted to withdraw but were unable to get away. The invaders began setting fire to the barracks and the occupants tried to escape. In the fracas, according to Thomas

Robinson of the Canadian militia, two of Walsh's men were killed. [6] The burning embers used to set fire to the barracks reportedly came from the fireplace of a Black man named Mills. One version claims that Mills shouted, "God save the Queen" or something similar, and was shot dead.Two adjacent houses burned with the barracks. Bierce's men also burned the steamer *Thames* docked nearby. While a messenger galloped to Sandwich to alert Lieutenant-Colonel Prince, Bierce read a proclamation that had been signed at Detroit by Samuel Lount's son William, the "military secretary" of the Hunters in the west, that called on Canadians to rise up. Then like the Gilbert and Sullivan creation, the Duke of Plaza Toro, Bierce proceeded to lead his men from behind, keeping his group close to the point where they had landed.

One of the other two groups had reached the centre of the village while the third (less than 150 men) had gone beyond to the Baby farm when the first of the troops reached Windsor. These were one company of 40 men called the Provincial Volunteer Militia, under Captain John Frederick Sparke (who had served as adjutant in Colonel Joseph Hill's Queen's Light Infantry), and a company led by Captain John Bell (previously of the Royal Kent Volunteers). Just behind them were three companies of the Essex militia.

These five companies actually fought the Battle of Windsor. Sparke's men were uniformed in the red coats with which, thus far, few of the militia had been issued and were well trained.[7] The battle took place in an orchard south and west of the Baby house. Sparke's company's accurate fire sent the invaders reeling. Meanwhile, part of the Essex militia flanked the intruders and caught them in their crossfire.

While this was going on, a militia officer and Dr. John Hume, an assistant surgeon, came rushing up from Sandwich to help. Finding Bierce's second company in the village, the two men ran, but Hume was hunted down and killed with an axe and a bayonet. At that point John Prince, "dressed in a fustian shooting coat and fur cap" rather than in uniform, arrived from Sandwich with a small reinforcement. He later stated that his entire force amounted to some 130 men. Uncertain of the enemy's strength or location, he ordered a retreat to Sandwich, then the more important centre, to await the arrival of regular troops from Fort Malden, whom he had sent for. Angry over the constant attacks and the death of his friend Dr. Hume, Prince ordered four prisoners summarily shot.

At about 11.00 a.m. Captain Edward Broderick arrived from Amherstburg with 100 men of the 34th regiment, accompanied by a gun and some artillerymen under Lieutenant Dionysius Airey (a brother of the lieutenant-colonel of the 34th) and forty to fifty Indians under George Ironside, an Indian agent. The regulars, militiamen and Indians then set out for Windsor looking for fleeing republicans. During the pursuit forty-four prisoners were taken. Prince had one more summarily executed, and he reported that twenty-one of the enemy had been killed [8]. Bierce and thirty others who had stayed a safe distance to the rear, retreated to the shore where they had landed, stole some canoes and got away to Hog Island (now Belle Island, Michigan). According to one account they were nearly caught by the American steamer *Erie*, sent by General Hugh Brady from Detroit. Another version claims that the *Erie* did in fact take into custody some of those trying to escape. Meanwhile, the regulars had joined the search, and one officer of the 34th who kept a diary recorded that they spotted half a dozen "rebels" pulling off in a boat:

> the field piece was immediately unlimbered and pointed against it. The range was a long one, about 1000 yards and the boat not far from the shore of Hogg [*sic*] Island. Airey however managed to get 5 shots at it before the men could gain the woods, all of the balls struck close to the boat and one of them, the third, took away a man's arm, who was conveyed on board the U.S. steamer *Erie* which had during the whole of the morning been cruising in the river to prevent the rebels taking refuge in the American territory. [9]

Among the forty-four captives were two of Duncombe's rebels, Paul Bedford of Norwich and Joshua Doan of Yarmouth. All were taken to Amherstburg by the regulars and sent to London for trial. Sir George Arthur ordered Colonel Charles Chichester, the unattached officer then at Chatham, to investigate the cold-blooded killing of the five prisoners, cautioning him to get "the information required, in a manner, the least calculated to wound Colonel Prince's feelings, which I wish to avoid...."

Suspecting that the attack on Windsor might be a feint, and a larger attack would be made on Amherstburg, Arthur ordered the three companies of the 85th Regiment, then in Toronto, to Gosfield Township, on the shore of Lake Erie. From there the troops could support the 34th in Amherstburg, should the attack materialize. One of Arthur's staff officers, Colonel Mackenzie Fraser, inspected the area and reported that there was no suitable accommodation at Gosfield. Sir George approved the construction of "Large Log Musket Proof Barracks" by some of the "Country People and the men themselves...." [10]

Arthur hurried to Windsor for a first-hand report, and he decided that the companies of the 85th Regiment, then en route from Toronto, would be stationed at Sandwich, where the accommodation was better. He had already resolved to deal harshly with the men captured on Canadian soil as a result of the border infractions. James Morreau, executed for his part in the Short Hills raid, had been tried by a district court, but the prisoners taken at Windsor, like those captured near Prescott, would face courts martial. By the time the Battle of Windsor was fought, 72 of the 131 prisoners taken at the

Battle of the Windmill were under sentence of death, and the 39 who were under-age had been convicted and pardoned. Arthur asked his Judges of the Court of Queen's Bench for advice on how the condemned men should be treated, and most recommended carrying out all the executions. One dissenter was Judge Levius Sherwood, who recommended hanging only the ringleaders, ten, or at most twelve of them. Replying to Arthur, Sherwood wrote:

> The agonizing suffering of the criminals never fails to excite pity in the general mass of the people, and such effects are always to be deprecated and particularly in all political offenses . . . I think such consequences are to be guarded against, as far as appears consistent with a vindication of the Majesty of the laws and a determined support of the constituted authorities.

Sherwood suggested transportation of the others to a penal colony, adding, "I think it would be impolitic to pardon even one of them."[11]

The trials at Kingston had started on 28 November, and the first defendant was Daniel George. His brother-in-law visited the young Kingston lawyer, John A. Macdonald, and asked him to defend the accused. Macdonald agreed, but when he learned that the trials were to be courts martial he informed George that he could not appear but could only advise him. Macdonald also met with Dorephus Abbey and Nils von Schoultz. The lawyer felt that George and Abbey were getting what they deserved, but like many others he was impressed by the handsome, personable self-professed Pole and taken in by the less than accurate details of his past.

A lagoon on Belle Island, part of the escape route for republicans fleeing from Windsor after the raid.

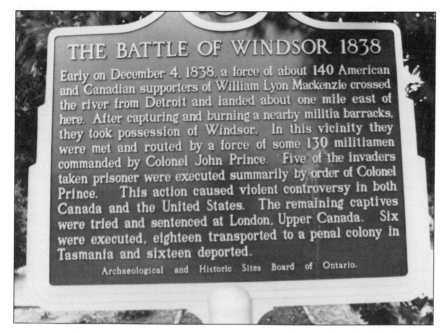

THE BATTLE OF WINDSOR 1838

Early on December 4, 1838, a force of about 140 American and Canadian supporters of William Lyon Mackenzie crossed the river from Detroit and landed about one mile east of here. After capturing and burning a nearby militia barracks, they took possession of Windsor. In this vicinity they were met and routed by a force of some 130 militiamen commanded by Colonel John Prince. Five of the invaders taken prisoner were executed summarily by order of Colonel Prince. This action caused violent controversy in both Canada and the United States. The remaining captives were tried and sentenced at London, Upper Canada. Six were executed, eighteen transported to a penal colony in Tasmania and sixteen deported.

Archaeological and Historic Sites Board of Ontario.

Plaque commemorating the Battle of Windsor that was erected in downtown Windsor. Prince actually arrived on the scene after the main skirmish had ended.

The thirty-one-year old von Schoultz insisted on pleading guilty and taking full responsibility for what had occurred at the windmill. After talking to him, Macdonald felt that he had been deluded, and begged him to throw himself on the mercy of the court. Von Schoultz refused to change his plea, and he was sentenced to hang on 8 December. Arthur allowed von Schoultz to be hanged at Fort Henry, rather than at the Kingston jail, and the execution took place as scheduled.[12] Dorephus Abbey and Daniel George were executed at the Kingston jail on 12 December, and Martin Woodruff followed on the 19th. On the 22nd Joel Peeler and Sylvanus Sweet went to the scaffold, and by this time, as Levius Sherwood had warned Arthur, the outcry over the hangings was becoming strident. On 4 January 1839, Christopher Buckley, Sylvester Lawton, Russel Phelps and Duncan Anderson met their deaths, while the eleventh and final execution, that of Leman Leach, took place on 11 February. The sentences of the other prisoners at Kingston were commuted to transportation to the penal colony at Van Diemen's Land.[13]

Leach's was the last execution for participation in the border raids. The courts martial of the forty-four men captured at Windsor had begun before the end of December in London. One man was acquitted, twenty-one were later deported to the United States, while sixteen were sentenced to transportation and six to death. The first man hanged was Hiram Lynn on 7 January, followed by Daniel Bedford on the 11th, Albert Clark on the 14th, Cornelius Cunningham on 4 February, and Joshua Doan and Amos Perley on the 6th. [14] Some months would pass before the prisoners sentenced to transportation were all moved to Quebec City for embarkation, and in the interval those not yet at Fort Henry were moved there.

Three of the executions contradict the popular illusion that families of U.E. Loyalist origin were unswervingly loyal during the rebellions and the raids by republicans. Joshua Doan, Amos Perley and Peter Matthews all sprang from such roots. None of those transported have been positively identified, but many who were arrested, especially in the Midland District, belonged to families who had chosen the King's side at the time of the American Revolution. The notion that all Loyalists' descendants in Upper Canada were loyal in 1837-1838 does not survive close scrutiny.

As the new year began, Arthur disembodied most of his sedentary militia. The return for 27 November showed that he had raised, in his incorporated and embodied units, 296 provincial artillerymen, 1,068 cavalrymen, and 18,294 infantrymen, a total strength of 19,658 all ranks. He retained the incorporated units — four regiments and Magrath's Queen's Lancers and the Black companies — the twelve provisional battalions, and the Independent Volunteer companies [15]. All told, some 8,000 men were discharged and allowed to return home.

By that time the other three companies of the 85th Regiment had arrived in Kingston and moved on to St. Thomas, and Colborne had dispatched the 93rd (Highland) Regiment of Foot to Toronto. These Highlanders, unlike the 73rd, wore the kilt and plaid in a variation of government (Black Watch) tartan. In place of the shako was a feathered bonnet with a band diced scarlet-green-white. They were commanded by Major Robert Spark, who was soon promoted to lieutenant-colonel. A further reinforcement sent to Kingston was three companies of the 65th (2nd Yorkshire North Riding) Regiment.

The number of regular troops in Upper Canada now amounted to more than 5,000 all ranks — eight regiments, half of the 65th, and the detachments of the King's Dragoon Guards and of the Royal Artillery. More regulars were in the province in 1814, but in 1838

Canada was not at war. Still, the militia provided the numbers, even after Arthur's reductions. Arthur now felt secure enough to permit the 24th Regiment to go to Quebec City for refitting. He was again requesting a separate commissariat department, but the Lords of Treasury in London did not think this was necessary. [16] Arthur had to be content with the thought that expenditures for the regulars would stimulate the province's economy.

The factions were showing no signs of reconciliation. To the subdued Reformers, the Family Compact seemed more firmly entrenched than before the rebellions. John Strachan, the leader of the oligarchy, had been appointed the first Anglican Bishop of Toronto in 1838 (to take effect in 1839). Marshall Spring Bidwell, one of the moderate Reformers, had moved to Albany, while Robert Baldwin was avoiding politics. Many of the radicals were in exile, or living nervously at home after release from jail, and worrying that their neighbours might attack them. People close to the frontiers feared that Arthur's stern measures might not be enough to dissuade the republicans from further mischief, and that his force of regulars and militia might not prevent the loss of innocent lives such as had occurred at Windsor.

Back in England, Lord Durham completed his famous report on conditions in the Canadas in January 1839. His most important recommendations were the granting of responsible government and the union of the two provinces under one legislature. When copies of the report arrived in March, the Tories were infuriated, because they saw any move towards responsible government as creeping republicanism. They were convinced that Durham was betraying the very people who had come forward to protect the British connection, and catering to traitors who wanted a republic. Reformers were pleased but cautious. Some organized what they called "Durham meetings" in honour of their champion, but they were circumspect. Tories were as ready to break up these meetings as they had those of the political unions of the autumn of 1837.

The militia remained at border posts; the regulars were for the most part at the various headquarters, ready to counter-attack if need arose. In spite of the many alarms, as an economy measure Arthur ordered a reduction in the number and size of his provisional battalions. By a Militia General Order of 13 April 1839, he advised his regimental commanders that from then on he would have only five provisional battalions, each of four companies, and all men who remained must be volunteers, a measure which he hoped would improve morale. Sir John Colborne ordered that full strength for each incorporated battalion be 500 all ranks. Sir Allan MacNab's 1st Battalion would be quartered at London; the 2nd, now under Brooke Young, would be posted to Chatham; the 3rd, William Kingsmill's, had recently moved to Chippawa; and the 4th under Joseph Hill was to remain in Kingston.

Colborne was alarmed that Arthur's return for 27 November had shown more than 1,000 provincial cavalrymen, and he hoped that the numbers could be reduced because of the heavy expense. Arthur's records revealed that the cost of maintaining Major Thomas Magrath's "troop" for one day was £18.11.10 Sterling, or £22. 6. 2 currency. This covered food and accommodation for ten officers, fifty privates, three infantrymen who were servants, three women, eight children, and sixty-three horses. [17]

While the courts martial of the prisoners taken at Windsor were being held, the republicans at Detroit staged an "indignation meeting" that was addressed by Edward Theller. Captured on the schooner *Anne* off Bois Blanc Island in January 1838, Theller had been moved to the citadel in Quebec City, but he escaped and returned to Detroit. At the meeting he declared that he would raise 2,000 men to invade Upper Canada, and would soon be "washing his hands in the blood of Colonel John Prince." Fearing more trouble, Arthur made a winter journey to Amherstburg to inspect the defences.

At Niagara, someone attempted to set fire to Sheriff Alexander Hamilton's house, while at Queenston a barn belonging to Dr. John Newburn was burnt. Newburn had presided over the inquest on the body of Captain Edgeworth Ussher after his murder. As the summer of 1839 progressed, more buildings along the Niagara River were put to the torch, one of them the Anglican church at Chippawa. The meetings of the republicans continued, with many threats. Armed men roamed the border areas of New York, Michigan and Ohio, but their pronouncements for the most part were bluff. Many of the incidents along the St. Lawrence involved shipping. On 14 April the steamer *United States* was fired on from Prescott, and for a time the ship stayed away from the river.

On 17 May a much more serious episode began in Brockville. At that time Colonel William Marshall, the unattached regular officer, was in command, and his garrison was still the detachment of the 73rd Regiment under Lieutenant William Hervey FitzGerald. The American schooner *G.F. Weeks* stopped at the wharf and on deck lay a 6-pounder cannon for Ogdensburg, to replace a gun stolen by the republicans before they went to Windmill Point. The master of the *Weeks* showed his bill of lading to the deputy collector of customs, Charles Prevost, who agreed that the gun was freight and gave his permission for goods destined for Brockville to be unloaded. Because some people noticed the gun, James Morris, one of the magistrates, went to the wharf to prevent anyone moving it before Colonel Marshall could arrange for a guard. Then Prevost's superior, Richard Duncan Fraser of Prescott, who was the collector of customs, arrived aboard the steamer *Brockville*. When people complained to him about the presence of the gun, Fraser ordered the *Weeks* seized, then he left for Fort Wellington, to resume his duties as colonel of the 2nd Grenville Regiment. Amidst cheers, some local men removed the gun from the schooner's deck and paraded through the town, firing it repeatedly, although as the *Recorder* reported, they only used blanks. Colonel Marshall arrived with his sentries, but was too late to prevent the seizure of the gun by what was now a mob. After posting the sentries to prevent any more thefts from the *Weeks*, both Marshall and Magistrate Morris withdrew.

At five o'clock on the afternoon of the 18th, a Saturday, the American steamer *Oneida* arrived off the blockhouse with Colonel William Worth and 100 United States regulars aboard. When Worth and a junior officer came ashore they were treated rudely and told not to land any of their soldiers on the wharf. At that moment Lieutenant FitzGerald of the 73rd Regiment reached the wharf and jumped aboard the steamer, which put out and drew in at another wharf. Lieutenant FitzGerald then conducted the American officers to Colonel Marshall's quarters. Marshall recommended that Worth confer with Colonel Fraser, since he was the collector of customs who had ordered the *Weeks* seized. The officers returned to the *Oneida* and sailed on to Prescott, where Worth showed Fraser the permits to unload, of which the latter was unaware. Fraser agreed to deliver up the gun and the schooner, and the *Oneida* returned to Brockville waters. The deputy collector of customs, Charles Prevost, could not get the gun away from the mob. Since the detachment of the 73rd Regiment was so small, Colonel Marshall sent a message to Kingston asking for reinforcements.

The steamers *Traveller* and *Kingston* arrived from Kingston bringing a company of regulars from the 83rd Regiment. The ringleaders were soon arrested and the gun was placed aboard the *Weeks*. The *Oneida* was ordered to leave Canadian waters, but the *Weeks* was unable to follow immediately because of contrary winds. Feeling in the town ran high because people disapproved of the way the gun had been retrieved. Colonel Worth had used gunboat diplomacy, for the *Oneida*, which was now armed, had patrolled offshore with colours flying. Meanwhile, Sir George Arthur learned of the fuss in Brockville. He wanted to inspect the entire St. Lawrence front, and he arrived off Brockville aboard the steamer *William IV* on the afternoon of Tuesday 21 May but he did not land. He transferred to the *Traveller* and continued on to Cornwall. He returned to Brockville on Saturday the 25th and came ashore, where he inspected the barracks and the artillery and received an address from 266 citizens who were furious at the way the cannon had been recovered. Colonel Worth had been high handed, and the British soldiers had no business assisting him. Arthur was inclined to agree with them, but he resolved on conciliation. He chided his subjects for placing him in an embarrassing predicament, and informed them that he had appealed to the United States government over the ill-judged conduct of Colonel Worth. [18]

Another incident took place on 4 August, near Brockville, when the American steam packet *St. Lawrence* was overtaken by the steamer *Montreal*, commanded by Lieutenant William Fowell. He demanded that the *St. Lawrence* show her colours, and when he was not obeyed he ordered his men to fire their muskets at her. [19] The Americans were making some attempt at conciliation themselves, for they arrested William Lyon Mackenzie. He had been indicted in Albany on 12 June 1838 for having invaded Upper Canada by trespassing on Navy Island. After several postponements he was finally tried at Canandaigua, New York, on 20 June 1839, fined ten dollars and sentenced to eighteen months in the Monroe County jail. He had barely been supporting his wife and children before his imprisonment, and afterwards they could scarcely eke out an existence. [20]

The other incarcerated rogue, Bill Johnston, escaped from Albany jail after serving six months of his one-year sentence, and with his daughter Kate he returned to the Clayton area. He was hiding among the Thousand Islands and hoping for a pardon from President Van Buren. (Not until President William Henry Harrison's brief time in office in 1841 did Johnston receive one.) [21]

While Sir George Arthur was still in Brockville, a conspiracy was hatching in a boarding house in Rochester that was kept by John Montgomery (after his escape from Fort Henry) — a meeting place for Canadian exiles. On 20 July 1839, a Friday, Samuel P. Hart, who had lived in Cobourg and Belleville (where he was a newspaper editor) before leaving the province, Benjamin Lett, Edward Kennedy and four others, boarded the schooner *Guernsey*

View of Cobourg in 1839-1841 about the time of the conspiracy against certain citizens. The large building in the middle background is the original Victoria College.

at Oswego. Late on Saturday the six were put ashore five miles east of Cobourg, taking with them a trunk filled with guns and bowie knives, bundles of matches and bottles of turpentine. The would-be assailants walked three miles towards the village, stopping at the farm of Joseph Ash. The visitors had ambitious schemes, and as usual they were expecting local support. Led by Samuel Hart, they planned to rob Maurice Jaynes, a wealthy farmer, and Robert Henry, who kept a private bank in his house on King Street, and to murder two members of the Family Compact, George S. Boulton and D'Arcy Boulton Jr. Then they intended stealing a schooner they had seen in the harbour for a hasty return to the American side. At the Ash farm another conspirator, Henry Moon, joined them.

Moon drew the line at murder, and on Monday morning he sneaked away from the Ash farm and warned D'Arcy Boulton of the plot. Boulton called a magistrate, who formed a posse and surrounded the Ash house. They captured Samuel Hart, Ash and his son, and three of the others who had come from Oswego, but not Benjamin Lett and Edward Kennedy. No reference was made to embodying local militia to hunt for Lett and Kennedy, but the schooner *Guernsey* was seized when it stopped at Port Credit.

On 1 August the magistrates of Cobourg sent a request for protection to Sir George Arthur, and repeated it on the 5th. On the 11th the steamer *Commodore Barrie* arrived from Hamilton bringing eighty men belonging to Sir Allan MacNab's first incorporated battalion. MacNab was reported to be in hot pursuit, but he was in London at the headquarters of his battalion. The detachment was led by Samuel Ussher, a brother of Edgeworth Ussher who was thought to have been murdered by Benjamin Lett. Arthur told Colborne that he sent a company of incorporated militia to Cobourg, and he may have chosen Samuel Ussher to lead it when he learned that the infamous Lett had been involved and was still at large. [22]

The six captives stood trial in Cobourg on 13 September before Judge Jonas Jones, and they were defended by one of their intended victims — D'Arcy Boulton Jr. All were found guilty, and Samuel Hart was sentenced to seven years in the penitentiary, the others to shorter terms or fines. At about the same time, some 100 fettered prisoners, captured mainly at Windsor and Prescott, began leaving Fort Henry in open boats, passing along the Rideau Canal bound for Montreal, the first stage of the journey that for most would end at the other side of the world in the penal colony of Van Diemen's Land. Nine, however, were released in England after a British court reviewed their cases. [23]

In October 1839, Charles Poulett Thomson, a civilian, arrived to take over the administration of Upper Canada, while Sir George Arthur remained as his deputy and the commander of forces. Thomson would prepare the province for the union with Lower Canada, as Lord Durham had recommended. The union was to be implemented in 1841, with Thomson as the governor general. In Toronto, Thomson was sworn in on 22 November. A few weeks before, Sir John Colborne retired and returned to England. His successor, and Arthur's superior, was Sir Richard Downes Jackson. [24]

Chapter 13
Denouement 1840-1850

C harles Poulett Thomson had no authority to implement responsible government. The Colonial Office was not yet ready to take such a step. Thomson's instructions for 1840 were to create a more efficient administration, but within the existing constitution. Soon after he was sworn in, he went on a tour of the upper province, leaving Sir George Arthur to carry on in Toronto and keep a weather eye on the frontiers.

In February 1840, Adjutant-General of Militia Richard Bullock reported that 10,000 uniforms were required for the militia infantry in Upper Canada. The coatees were to be red, faced blue with white lace for the rank and file, silver for the officers. The enlisted men (other ranks) would have shakos, forage caps and belts, the sergeants red sashes, the officers swords. Uniform buttons would be engraved with "V R" surmounted with a crown and the words "Upper Canadian Militia". Other items on Bullock's list included greatcoats, boots, knapsacks, mess tins, haversacks, stocks and clasps, and thirty bugles. [1] Acting on orders from the now departed Sir John Colborne, Arthur established a fifth regiment of incorporated militia, to be raised in the Cornwall area, and he appointed Philip VanKoughnett the lieutenant-colonel commandant. Thomson, at that time touring in the Eastern District, had an interview with Colonel Donald Macdonell (Greenfield) of the 2nd Glengarry Regiment, who was very disappointed that the command of the new regiment had not gone to him. Thomson wrote to Arthur suggesting that he reconsider his choice, "As the Highland Blood seems amazingly excited at the prospect of being commanded again by a Dutchman." Arthur explained that he did not want Macdonell, for VanKoughnett was the better administrator, and more careful with public money. Macdonell had accumulated a regimental debt of £300 that was still owing from the autumn of 1838 when he had taken his Glengarries to Lower Canada. Arthur left VanKoughnett in command of the new regiment, but he agreed that should the Glengarries be required again in Lower Canada, Macdonell, an excellent field commander, would lead them.[2] On 14 February,

Charles Poulett Thomson, 1st Baron Sydenham, first governor of the United Province of Canada that was established in 1841.

Arthur's incorporated militia stood at 3,500 infantry and Major Magrath's cavalry at 50. [3]

A return for the regulars dated 1 March 1840 showed how they were distributed:

Sandwich: Captain Herbert Taylor with 139 rank and file of the 85th Regiment.

Amherstburg: Lieutenant-Colonel Richard Airey with 507 of the 34th Regiment, 15 Royal Artillery and 10 Royal Sappers and Miners.

London: Lieutenant-Colonel James Frederick Love with 553 of the 73rd Regiment, 336 of the 85th, and 43 Royal Artillery.

Drummondville: Major James Forlong and 549 of the 43rd Regiment (Lieutenant-Colonel Henry Booth was ill), 35 Royal Artillery and 7 King's Dragoon Guards.

Niagara: Captain Richard Martin and 82 King's Dragoon Guards, and 8 Royal Artillery.

Toronto: Major-General Sir George Arthur, Lieutenant-Colonel William Cuthbert Ward of the Royal Engineers, with 551 rank
and file of the 32nd Regiment, 578 of the 93rd, and 89 Royal Artillery.

Kingston:Lieutenant-Colonel Henry Dundas with 530 of the 83rd Regiment, 188 of the 65th, and 130 Royal Artillery.

Prescott: Lieutenant-Colonel William Freke Williams (unattached) with 8 Royal Artillery and 29 of the 65th Regiment.

Penetanguishene: Fort Adjutant James Keating.

Bytown (Ottawa): Major Daniel Bolton of the Royal Engineers.

The total regular force amounted to 4,399 all ranks, while 279 women, 655 children, and 46 servants who were not soldiers were "Drawing Rations." An allowance was being paid for forage for 360 riding and draft horses.[4]

Arthur wanted to remove the 43rd Regiment from the Niagara frontier, where it had been stationed since July 1838. The logical replacement for Drummondville was the 93rd Regiment, which thus far had remained at Toronto. But he had misgivings about placing Highlanders on that particular frontier, as "They are generally farming men; and, at a short distance from the Niagara frontier is a Scotch settlement from whence I have not a doubt many allurements will be held out".[5] Despite his suspicions he did send the 93rd to Drummondville, and the 43rd was moved to Amherstburg.

Sir George issued a Militia General Order on 16 April authorizing a limited incorporated militia to continue on duty for two years, commencing on 1 May. Each of the five incorporated regiments would be reduced to four companies and a total of 288 privates. The headquarters for the 1st incorporated would be at

The steamer *William IV* which plied the waters from 1832 until 1858. Drawing by C.H.J. Snider after one by William J. Thomson.

Hamilton, at Sandwich for the 2nd, at Niagara for the 3rd, at Prescott for the 4th, and at Cornwall for the 5th. (later the 4th would be moved to Cornwall and replaced at Prescott by the 5th.) The order included a reprimand to certain militiamen who had carried a "Party Banner" through communities along the St. Lawrence. Arthur forbade such practices as "bad for harmony."[6] The militia was not to interfere in politics.

Later in April, some republicans infiltrated the Niagara frontier above Queenston and set a charge of explosives that destroyed the top of the Brock Monument. The perpetrators were never identified, although Benjamin Lett was suspected of being back of this senseless act. Afterwards, Ogden Creighton's stables near the Falls and some farm buildings were burnt, as more warnings of attack were sent from Buffalo.[7]

On 10 May, William Lyon Mackenzie was released from jail, and afterwards he moved his family to New York City — events that attracted little attention in Upper Canada. The standing army was preoccupied with the ongoing Maine-New Brunswick boundary

dispute. Sir George Arthur was worried that the controversy might spark renewed violence. In August, Sir Richard Downes Jackson, Colborne's successor in Lower Canada, sent the refitted 24th Regiment to Kingston by steamer to reinforce the 83rd and the three companies of the 65th. However, the garrison of regulars was enlarged only temporarily. A few weeks later the 73rd and the 85th were withdrawn to Montreal. The 24th was the replacement for one of them, while the replacement for the other was the second battalion of the 1st (Royal) Regiment of Foot commanded by Lieutenant-Colonel George Augustus Wetherall.

The War Office returns refer to Wetherall's battalion as the "2nd B the Royal", which has led to some confusion over its identity. The 24th Regiment remained at Kingston, and Wetherall took the "Royals" to London. The parade ground at London, Sir George Arthur informed Lieutenant-Colonel John Eden, the Deputy Adjutant-General in Quebec City, needed a gravel surface. The sand that had been laid down originally was very fine, and the men's boots stirred up such clouds of dust that too many soldiers were suffering from

The steamer *St. Lawrence,* which was fired on by British troops when she failed to show her colours. Drawn by C.H.J. Snider.

H.M.S. *Mohawk,* in 1842, which operated on Lakes Huron and Erie until 1852. Drawing by C.H.J. Snider.

"ophthalmia" — in modern usage, conjunctivitis.

In September, Arthur reported to the new colonial secretary, Lord John Russell, that after some reductions because of expired enlistments, he had above 6,000 men in his garrison — seven regiments of the line (the Royals, 24th, 32nd, 34th, 43rd, 83rd and 93rd; he omitted the detachment of the 65th) and five regiments of incorporated militia, four batteries of artillery, two companies of King's Dragoon Guards, and one troop of provincial dragoons (Magrath's).[8] In 1840 the British government authorized the raising of the Royal Canadian Rifle Regiment from among veterans serving in Canada who had been a minimum of 15 years in a regular regiment. Since veterans were entitled to pensions after sixteen years of service, they would be less prone to desertion and could be used to man frontier posts. To protect the shores, three more armed steamers were built — HMS *Minos* at Chippawa to serve on Lake Erie, and the *Cherokee* and the *Mohawk* at Kingston for Lake Ontario and the upper St. Lawrence. [9]

Governor Thomson, in the meantime, was busy with the civil administration. In order to secure the cooperation of the elected representatives, Thomson hinted that the capital of the united province would be west of the Ottawa River. Once he got what he

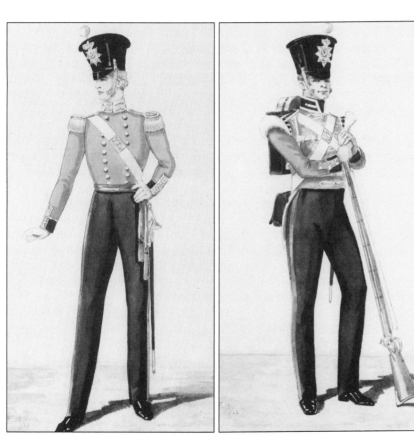

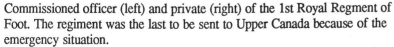

Commissioned officer (left) and private (right) of the 1st Royal Regiment of Foot. The regiment was the last to be sent to Upper Canada because of the emergency situation.

Private (left) and captain (right) in the 71st Regiment of Foot.

wanted from the members of the legislature, he announced that his seat of government would be Kingston, to the consternation of the people of Toronto. The governor was adamant. Toronto had been blessed with the financial stimulus the capital had provided since 1793, but Kingston, with a population of some 7,000, had been stagnating and needed the benefit the seat of government could bring. There, some stone cottages were renovated for government offices, and a new hospital building was taken over for the legislature. Alwington House was leased from Charles William Grant, the Baron of Longueuil, as a governor's residence. Thomson was created 1st Baron Sydenham for the work he had done to prepare Upper Canada for union, which would come into effect on 1 January 1841.

By December 1840 the campaign for the general election that would follow the union was under way, and again Arthur had to step in to check interference by the militia in politics. At Hamilton the Reformers were alarmed by Lieutenant-Colonel MacNab's incorporated militiamen. Arthur hastily made a plan to exchange MacNab's 1st regiment with VanKoughnett's 5th Regiment from Cornwall, "to get rid of Sir Allan's Tory Militia supporters if possible". On second thought, Arthur decided that moving the men and their families so great a distance so late in the year would entail hardship. Instead, he exchanged MacNab's regiment with William Kingsmill's 3rd Regiment, then on duty at Queenston, Chippawa, Fort Erie and Port Colborne. [10]

In England the Board of Ordnance was alarmed at the mounting cost of defence, and the secretary had informed Lord Russell on 18 February that the Canadians ought to be able to defend themselves, with some support from regular troops. The Duke of Wellington, however, felt that Britain should protect a people who had demonstrated, by crushing the rebellions, that they wanted to maintain the British connection. Yet if the mother country was not prepared to defend these colonists, the Duke thought that they should be abandoned at once so that they could drive some suitable bargain with the United States. [11]

The 43rd Regiment was at Amherstburg, the "Royals" and most of the 83rd were at London with a detachment of the latter at St. Thomas; the 93rd and one squadron of the King's Dragoon Guards remained on the Niagara frontier; the 32nd and half of the 34th were at Toronto; the 24th and the other half of the 34th were at Kingston, as were most of the Royal Artillery. Drawing rations were 237 women and 738 children.

In addition to the five regiments of incorporated militia, which were really provincial regulars, Colonel Colley Foster's returns showed 1,651 embodied militia and volunteers — 303 in the London and Western Districts under Lieutenant-Colonel Wetherall of the 1st Royal; 659 in the London and Gore Districts under Lieutenant-Colonel Robert Spark of the 93rd; 38 in the Home District under Sir George Arthur; and 651 at Kingston and along the St. Lawrence under Lieutenant-Colonels Alexander Maclachlan of the Royal Artillery at Kingston and William Freke Williams at Prescott.

Foster's report, dated 18 March 1841, included figures on desertion, which must have applied mainly to the regulars. Since 23 March 1838, 467 men had deserted, while 141 had been tried for desertion. Whether the 141 were included in 467 was not clear, but if 467 actually deserted and were not retaken, that number implied the loss of virtually an entire battalion. [12] Such losses explain Colborne's concern about deserters, and his wish to station regulars away from border posts.

Sir George Arthur's tour of duty ended in May 1841, and he left for home, where he was created a baronet for his services. Lord Sydenham's days were numbered, for he shattered a leg in a fall from his horse and died soon afterwards. He was buried in St. George's Cathedral in Kingston. His successor was Sir Charles Bagot, who had negotiated the Rush-Bagot Agreement in 1818.

That September of 1841 the republicans contemplated their final outrage. A report that they planned to blow up some locks on the Welland Canal reached Lieutenant-Colonel Spark at Drummondville. By rushing regulars from his 93rd Regiment to the scene, embodying local militia and informing the officers of the Black companies at Chippawa, the attempt was foiled.[13]

In 1842 the number of regulars in the united province peaked at 12,452 all ranks. Tension relaxed after 9 August with the signing of the Webster-Ashburton Treaty that settled the Maine — New Brunswick boundary dispute. In September three regiments of regulars were withdrawn from Lower Canada (the names Canada East and Canada West were not used in military reports). Then in January 1843, Sir Charles Bagot recommended disbanding all the provincial troops, except for a corps of 100 Blacks to remain in the vicinity of the Welland Canal, and three troops of cavalry, in all 120 men, to patrol sensitive parts of the border of the united province. The Black corps was placed under the command of Captain

Alexander MacDonald, a former officer in the Frontier Light Infantry. [14] After that unit was disbanded, MacDonald had led a Black company at Chippawa. Final disbandment of some of the incorporated regiments did not take place until 1850, for the relaxation of tension with the United States was short-lived because of the Oregon boundary dispute of 1846.

By that time some Canadian exiles were being offered amnesty, and some had begun returning, while Dr. Charles Duncombe, Dr. John Rolph, David Gibson, Nelson Gorham and John Montgomery were pardoned. All but Duncombe returned home, Rolph to become a founder of the Canadian Medical Academy.[15] The sentences of the men transported to Van Diemen's Land were soon reduced and they began leaving the penal colony, if they could secure passage since neither money nor passage was provided. Most went to the United States, but a few returned to Canada.

Two major changes occurred simultaneous to the appointment of Lord Elgin, a son-in-law of Lord Durham, as governor general in September of 1846. Britain was finding the cost of defence prohibitive, and a new Whig ministry in the mother country was more willing to grant Canada self-government than its Tory predecessor. When Lord Elgin arrived in January 1847, his instructions were to act only as Queen Victoria's representative. Therefore the appointed governor no longer had any executive power, which meant that responsible government was now a fact. Implicit was the assumption that Canada could do with fewer regular troops and take more responsibility for her own defence.

The election of March 1848 brought the Reform Party to power, led by Robert Baldwin and Louis LaFontaine. This ministry soon passed the Rebellion Losses Bill that would compensate not only those who had been loyal, but the rebels in Lower Canada as well. The Conservatives were dismayed and they expected that Lord Elgin would withhold Royal assent.

While the bill was being debated and going through readings in February 1849, the Baldwin-LaFontaine ministry also issued a pardon to William Lyon Mackenzie, the last of the rebels of 1837 to go unpardoned. The little rebel decided to act on it, for he was a disillusioned soul who found that residence in a republic had not lived up to his expectations. He had written his son James, "I frankly confess to you that had I passed nine years in the United States before, instead of after, the outbreak of the Upper Canadian

Sir Charles Bagot, governor of the United Province of Canada from September 1841 until his death in 1843. The portrait was first published in 1844.

General Brock's monument above Queenston ca. 1834, based on a work by W.H Bartlett. The monument is shown intact.

Rebellion, I would have been the last man in America to engage in it." Mackenzie left New York City, and visited the Canadas to test the climate for his return. Stopping in Montreal, he went into the Parliamentary Library. John Prince, attending the session of the legislature, recognized him and recorded in his diary on 28 February 1849, " I turned William Lyon Mackenzie, the Traitor, out of the Library." When Mackenzie reached his brother-in-law's house in Toronto, a mob gathered outside and threatened to lynch him. [16] In 1850, however, Mackenzie was able to return to Toronto, get elected to parliament, and live out his life under the new form of government; as it turned out, he did not like it much better than the old.

On 25 April 1849, Lord Elgin gave Royal assent to the Rebellion Losses Bill, as was his duty. A riot broke out and the governor general's carriage was pelted with rotten eggs as he drove through the streets of Montreal. Although the mob burned the Parliament Building later that night, the bill signalled the close of the whole rebellion-republican — so-called patriot — era.

What the two Upper Canadian rebellions achieved is a matter of debate. A popular misconception is that because of the rebellions in the Canadas, Lord Durham was sent out, and Britain granted responsible government because he advised it. Yet Durham spent little time in Upper Canada, and his report was devoted largely to the situation in Lower Canada. Besides, the home government did not accept Durham's recommendation immediately. Eight years passed before Britain relented and withdrew the governor general's executive function. Nova Scotia, which did not have a rebellion, was given responsible government two months sooner than the united Canada, implying that the rebellions achieved nothing whatever. [17]

More significant was the effect the Upper Canadian rebellions had on certain residents of the United States. Men who joined Hunters' Lodges were eager to assist the supposedly downtrodden Upper Canadians achieve their freedom from Britain, and in the process to acquire land for landless American invaders, perhaps even to unite Upper Canada with the United States.The build-up of regular troops in Lower Canada was directed to a large extent against the people living there; in Upper Canada it was directed almost entirely against Americans and Canadian exiles who staged the border raids. The large number of killed, executed, and transported American and Canadian invaders demonstrated that most Upper Canadians were far from eager to be "freed" in this way. At the same time, the cost of maintaining a standing army in the Canadas probably influenced the mother country to grant responsible

General Brock's monument as it looked in 1844 before restoration work had begun. Drawing by Titus Hibbert, dated 10 October.

Trinity Anglican Church, Chippawa ca. 1913. The church had been rebuilt after the damage it sustained at the hands of the republicans.

New Fort York at Toronto. The fort was built during the 1840s on what are now the grounds of the Canadian National Exhibition. Known as The Stanley Barracks, only one building remains.

government far more than did the rebellions, particularly in the case of Upper Canada.

Evidence is found in the size of the regular force in the united province by 1854, which was reduced almost to the level of October 1837. On the eve of the rebellions the number of regulars in both provinces was about 3,350, of which some 600 were in Upper Canada. On 1 January 1854 the number was some 3,500, and 900 were in the upper province. [18] The reduction was not caused by Britain's involvement in the Crimean War, since the mother country did not declare war on Russia until March.

The two Upper Canadian rebellions have been called a farce and sometimes a comic opera. Certainly some of the episodes were comedy, yet with serious overtones. Both rebellions were accompanied by loss of lives. Good men died in the skirmishing, and some who perished at the end of the hangman's rope should never have had to make that sacrifice. That the executions of Matthews and Lount aroused such mixed feelings was shown by the numbers who signed petitions for clemency. Yet Lount, widely respected as a kindly man and a good neighbour, had led armed men. He must have known that the arms would be used. Public sentiment also curtailed the number of American and Canadian raiders who were put to death, as Judge Sherwood predicted.

Many of the dead on both sides left wives and children to fend for themselves at a time when social welfare was almost unknown. If the rebellions brought suffering, followed by bitterness and suspicion, the border raids were far more damaging. The terrorists who crossed the border after the two rebellions created , by their actions, a sense of fear, which sometimes bordered on panic among civilians. Terrorism was no more acceptable in the 1830s than it is 150 years after the events.

The Murney tower at Kingston. Three other large martello towers and two smaller ones were built in the 1840s to reinforce the defences at the foot of Lake Ontario.

James Bruce, 8th Earl of Elgin, the first governor-general who acted purely as the Queen's representative. Unlike his predecessors, Elgin had no executive power.

NOTES

Abbreviation

OA Ontario Archives
PAC Public Archives of Canada
MTPL Metropolitan Toronto Public Library
PRO Public Record Office, London, England

Notes to Chapter 1

1. Richard B. Howard, *Colborne's Legacy: Upper Canada College 1829-1979* (Toronto 1979) pp. 34-36.
2. Dennis Duffy, "Two Wars Struggling to Form the Conscience of a Single State". Address to the United Empire Loyalists' Association of Canada, Toronto, 25 May 1979.
3. PAC MG13 WOl7, vol. 1541, reel B-1577, pp. 145-161.
4. Sir Richard Bonnycastle, *The Canadas in 1841*, 2 vols. reprint (New York, 1968), vol. 1, p. 261.
5. PAC RGl, 14 May 1788, draft plan for new districts.
6. Brig. E.A. Cruikshank. *The Thirteenth Battalion of Infantry* (Hamilton 1899) p. 6.
7. J. Mackay Hitsman, *The Incredible War of 1812* (Toronto 1965) pp. 36-7.
8. Ontario Historical Society, Edith Firth ed., *Profiles of a Province* (Toronto 1967): George W. Spragge, "The Districts of Upper Canada 1788-1849," pp. 34-42. Colin Read, *The Rising in Western Upper Canada: The Duncombe Revolt and After* (Toronto 1982) p. 103.
9. PAC MGl3 WOl3 contains 44 volumes (Nos. 3673-3716) listing the members of the Upper Canadian Militia between 1837 and 1842. Some of the lists are not accurate. Certain officers named did little, while some not on the lists were among the most active ones.
10. Samuel Strickland, *Twenty-Seven Years in Canada West*, 2 vols., reprint (Edmonton 1970) vol. 2, p. 261.
11. Read, *The Rising*, p. 94, Deposition of William Storey, Decemberr 1837, from the Records of the London District Magistrates in the PAC.

Notes to Chapter 2

1. William Kilbourn, *The Firebrand: William Lyon Mackenzie and the Rebellion in Upper Canada* (Toronto 1956). Kilbourn's book is the most recent biography from which this brief summary is drawn. See also *Dictionary of Canadian Biography*, Vol IX, pp. 496-510
2. PAC RG lE3 vol. 42, pp. 236-237, Sherwood to Arthur, 10 Dec. 1838.
3. William Johnston, *History of Perth County 1825-1902* (Stratford 1903) p. 37.
4. Elinor Kyte Senior, *Redcoats and Patriotes: The Rebellions in Lower Canada 1837-38* (Canadian War Museum Historical Publication no. 20, Ottawa 1985) pp. 44-46, 55, 150.
5. Charles R. Sanderson ed., *The Arthur Papers* (Toronto: Toronto Public Libraries 1957) 3 volumes, vol. 1, #336, p. 288, Colborne to Arthur, 28 Sept. 1838.
6. Bonnycastle, *The Canadas in 1841* , vol. 2, pp. 63-64.
7. Sanderson, *Arthur Papers*, vol. 2, #756, pp. 135-142, report on the districts May 1839.
8. Gerald M. Craig, *Upper Canada: the Formative Years 1784-1841* (Toronto 1963) pp. 241-244.
9. Colin Read and Ronald J. Stagg, T*he Rebellion of 1837 in Upper Canada.* Champlain Society (Toronto 1985) pp. lvi-lvii, 123, item Bl2.
10. Sanderson, *Arthur Papers*, vol. 2, #765, p. 142.
11. Read, *Rising*, p. 57.
12. OA "Upper Canada Sundries", microfilm, item dated 11 Feb. 1839.
13. Edwin C. Guillet, *The Lives and Times of the Patriots* (Toronto 1968 edition) p. 9.
14. James FitzGibbon, *An Appeal to the People of the Late Province of Upper Canada* (Montreal, 24 May 1847) pp. 9-10.
15. Sir Richard Bonnycastle, *Canada as it Was, Is and May Be* (London 1852) 2 vols., vol. 1, pp. 201,259-261.

Notes to Chapter 3

1. Egerton Ryerson, *The Story of my Life* (Toronto 1883) p. 176.
2. FitzGibbon, *Appeal*, pp. 12-113.
3. Ibid.. pp. 14-15; John S. Moir, "FitzGibbon's Secret Visitor". *Ontario History*, vol. 48 (1956) pp. 108-110.
4. Guillet, *The Lives*, p. 15.
5. FitzGibbon, *Appeal*, pp. 15, 24.
6. J.K. Johnson, "The Social Composition of the Toronto Bank Guard 1837-1838," *Ontario History*, vol. 64 (1972) p. 97.
7. Patricia W. Hart, *Pioneering in North York* (Toronto 1968) pp. 67,161
8. FitzGibbon, *Appeal*, pp. 16-17.

9. Read and Stagg, *The Rebellion*, pp. 136-139, item B 20, John Powell's account, Toronto, 14 Feb. 1838.
10. FitzGibbon, *Appeal*, p. 18.
11. Kilbourn, *Firebrand*, p. 189.
12. FitzGibbon, *Appeal*, p. 19.
13. Andrew F. Hunter, *The History of Simcoe County*, the Historical Committee of Simcoe County (Barrie, 1890) reprint 1948, part 1, p. 275.
14. James Scott, *The Settlement of Huron County* (Toronto 1966) pp. 27-28.
15. Isabel Champion ed., *Markham 1795-1900*, Markham District Historical Museum (Markham 1979) p. 212; E.A. Cruikshank, "A Memoir of the Honourable James Kerby," *The Welland County Historical Society Papers and Records*, vol. 4 (Welland 1931) p. 228; Guillet, *The Lives*, p. 23; J.K. Johnson, 'Sir James Gowan, Sir John A. Macdonald and the Rebellion of 1837,' *Ontario History*, vol. 60 (1968) p. 62.
16. FitzGibbon, *Appeal*, p. 25.
17, Ruth McKenzie, *James FitzGibbon: Defender of Upper Canada* (Toronto 1983) p. 135.

Notes to Chapter 4

1. James FitzGibbon, *Narrative on the Occurrences in Toronto, Upper Canada in December 1837* (Toronto 13 Dec. 1837) pp. 14-16.
2. Guillet, *The Lives*, p. 24; Ruth McKenzie, *FitzGibbon*, pp. 137-139.
3. Guillett, *The Lives*, pp. 24, 25 fn. 12.
4. FitzGibbon, *Appeal*, p. 24.
5. Ibid., *Narrative*, p. 16
6. Ibid., *Appeal*, p. 29
7. Guillet, *The Lives*, p. 26, see also fn. 16.
8, Hunter, *Simcoe County*, pt. 1, p. 275.
9. Cruikshank, *Kerby Memoir*, pp. 128-129.
10. Guillet, *The Lives*, p..28, quoted from Mackenzie's narrative published in the Toronto *Examiner* 6 Oct. 1847.
11. Hazel K. Mathews, *Oakville and the Sixteen*. The Champlain Society (Toronto 1953) pp. 155, 156.
12. Scott, *Huron County*, p. 75.
13. PAC MG13 WO17, no. 1541, pp. 149, 157.
14. Bonnycastle, *Canada as It Was*, vol. 1, pp. 310-313.
15. PAC, Colborne Papers, Philpotts to Colborne, 4, 11 and 12 Dec. 1837, nos. 3111, 3141, 3161.
16. Ibid., MG27 1E30, Ferguson Papers, vol. 5., Ogle Robert Gowan, 'Memoirs of the Rebellions in Canada in 1837 and 1838.' Scrapbook and clippings from Gowan's newspaper *The Statesman*, pp. 11-16.
17. A memoir written by Kingsmill's granddaughter is preserved by the Kingsmill family.
18. Robert P. Bonis ed., *A History of Scarborough* (Scarborough 1968) p. 70.
19. Guillet, *The Lives,* pp. 34, 36, 41.

Notes to Chapter 5

1. Read, *The Rising*, Chapter 4. "The Revolt", pp. 82-106. Read's treatment is comprehensive and well documented, and his book was the first to concentrate on the events in the London District.
2. Ibid. p. 62.
3. Ibid. pp. 68-69.
4. Guillet, *The Lives*, p. 50.
5. PAC RG9 1Bl. Correspondence of the Adjutant-General's Office, vol. 34, Racey to Coffin, 8 Dec. 1837.
6. Read, *The Rising*, p. 95.
7. Leo A. Johnson, *History of Guelph 1827-1927*. Guelph Historical Society (Guelph 1977) p. 59.
8. PAC RG9 1Bl, vol. 34, Burwell to Joseph, 10 Dec. 1837.
9. Read, *The Rising*, pp. 96-97.
10. Ibid. pp. 89, 223-224.
11. Ibid. p. 98.
12. OA, Lieutenant Governor's Letter Books, Joseph to W.J. Kerr, 19 Dec. 1837.
13. OA, Upper Canada State Papers, vol. 45, p. 138, Petition of Lossing, 12 July 1838; Newspaper Collection, Toronto *Patriot*, 22 Dec. 1837, MacNab to Halkett, 15 Dec. 1837.
14. Read, *The Rising*, p. 101.
15. Sanderson, Arthur Papers, The index shows twenty-five references to claims unpaid from Head's time in office.
16. Read, *The Rising*, p. 102.
17. OA, Lieutenant Governor's Letter Books, 14 Dec. 1837.
18. OA, Newspaper Collection, Hamilton *Gazette*, 2 Jan. 1838.
19. Read, The Rising, p. 103.
20. PAC RG9 1Bl, vol. 24. Records of the Adjutant-General's Office, References to the Coloured Companies are dated from 24 Jan. to 2 Feb.1838.
21. Marion MacRae, *MacNab of Dundurn* (Toronto 1971) p. 86.

22. Read, *The Rising*, p. 106.
23. Fred Landon, *Western Ontario and the American Frontier* (reprinted Toronto 1962) p. 169.

Notes to Chapter 6

1. Cruikshank, *Kerby Memoir*, p. 128
2. Ibid., pp. 123-130.
3. PAC, RG9 lBl, vol. 22, Head to MacNab, 23 Dec. 1837.
4. Ibid., MG 24 A40, vol. 11, nos. 3265, 3267, 23 and 24 Dec. 1837.
5. Daniel G. Hill, *The Freedom Seekers: Blacks in Early Canada* (Agincourt, Ontario 1981) p. 121.
6. Guillet, *The Lives*, p. 77 and fn.
7. *The Dictionary of Canadian Biography,* vol. 10, pp. 482-483, Biography of Alexander McLeod.
8. Cruikshank, *Thirteenth Battalion*, p. 27.
9. Guillet, *The Lives*, p. 80.
10. Ibid., p. 81.
11. Cruikshank, *Thirteenth Battalion*, p. 28.
12. Guillet, *The Lives*, p. 83.
13. Ibid., pp. 153-154; 163, 259-63; the last is a list of the men on Navy Island; *The Dictionary of Canadian Biography*, vol. 11, p. 412, Biography of William Johnston.
14. OA, Newspaper Collection, *Upper Canada Gazette*, 28 Dec. 1837.
15. PAC, RG9 lBl, vol. 22, Militia General Orders of 27-28 Dec. 1837; Gowan "Memoir" p. 33; OA, Newspaper Collection, *Upper Canada Gazette*, 1 February 1838
16. OA, Newspaper Collection, *Upper Canada Gazette*, 4 Jan., 18 Jan. 1838.
17. Ibid., Colley Foster Papers, Letter to Mrs. Foster, 30 Dec.1837.
18. PAC, Colborne Papers, no. 3579-81, MacNab to Head, 11 Jan. 1838; Cruikshank, *Kerby Memoir*, p. 141.
19. Guillet, *The Lives*, p. 86.

Notes to Chapter 7

1. Guillet, *The Lives*, p. 88. Quoted from Theller's own account, *Canada in 1837-38*. 2 vols. (Philadelphia 1841).
2. R. Alan Douglas, *John Prince*, The Champlain Society (Toronto 1980) p. 15; Read and Stagg, *Rebellion*, Prince to John Joseph, 15 Dec. 1837.
3. Hill, *Freedom Seekers*, p. 118; PAC, RG9 lB2, vol. 17.

4. Read, *The Rising*, pp. 116, 120.
5. PAC, Gowan "Memoirs", pp. 36-37.
6. Guillet, *The Lives*, p. 90.
7. PAC, Colborne Papers, no. 3558, Colborne to Head, 8 Jan. 1838; OA, Newspaper Collection, *Upper Canada Gazette*, 11 Jan. 1838.
8. Michael Balthorp, *British Infantry Uniforms Since 1660* (Blandford Press, Poole, Dorset, England 1982) pp. 69, 74-75, 150. PAC, MGl3 WOl7, vol. 1541, p. 149.
9. Frederick Myatt, *The British Infantry 1660-1945* (Blandford Press, Poole, Dorset, England 1983) p. 106.
10. Senior, *Redcoats and Patriotes*, p. 150.
11. Sanderson, *Arthur Papers*, vol. 1, no. 139, p. 89.
12. Cruikshank, *Kerby Memoir*, p. 143; PAC RG9 lBl, vol. 24, Kerby's letter of 20 Jan. 1838.
13. Ibid. RG9 lBl, vol. 26. Hill's letters from Fort George began on 29 Jan. 1838.
14. Ibid. RG9 lB2, vol. 27. Daily State of the Incorporated Militia, Toronto, 5 Feb. 1838.
15. Cruikshank, *Kerby Memoir*, pp. 148, 150; OA, Newspaper Collection, *Upper Canada Gazette*, 26 Apr. 1838, Militia General Order.
16. Bonnycastle, *Canada as It Was*, vol. 2, pp. 73-74.
17. Ibid. p. 94.
18, Ibid. pp. 314-315.
19. Cruikshank, *Kerby Memoir*, p. 150.
20. Read, *The Rising*, pp. 122-123; J.P. Martyn, "The Patriot Invasion of Pelee Island", *Ontario History*, vol. 56(Sept. 1964), pp. 153-165. Most of the detail is drawn from the latter source.
21. Martyn, "The Patriot Invasion" p. 158.
22. Ibid. p. 159.
23. PAC, Gowan "Memoirs" p. 42; Douglas, *John Prince*, p. 21, no.61, from Prince's diary 4 Mar. 1838; no. 62, from Henry Rudyerd's diary 4 Mar. 1838.

Notes to Chapter 8

1. Sir Francis Bond Head, *The Emigrant* (London , 1846), pp. 261-287.
2. Craig, *Upper Canada*, pp. 252-254.
3. Read, *The Rising*, pp. 112-114.
4. Guillet, *The Lives*, pp. 63-66.
5. PAC, Colonial Office Records, CO 42, vol. 446, p. 51-53. Arthur to Glenelg,

14 Apr. 1838.

6. Ibid. RG9 IB1, vol. 23, orders for 6 Mar. 1838.
7. Ibid. Colborne Papers, no. 8065, n.d., Militia General Order.
8. Ibid. MG 13 WOl7, vol. 1542, p. 91.
9. Ibid. RG9 IB1, vol. 23, orders for 30 Apr. 1838.
10. Ibid. MG 13 WOl7, vol. 1542, p. 88.
11. Sanderson, *Arthur Papers*, vol. 1, no. 286, p. 257, Colborne to Arthur, 16 Aug. 1838.
12. K.R. Macpherson, "A List of Vessels Employed on British Service on the Great Lakes 1755-1857." *Ontario History*, vol. 55 (1963) pp. 178-179.
13. Cruikshank, *Kerby Memoir*, pp. 187-188.
14. Thad. W.H. Leavitt, *History of Leeds and Grenville Ontario From 1749 to 1875* (Brockville 1879) p. 44; Guillet, *The Lives*, p. 157.
15. Ibid. p. 158.
16. PAC, Gowan "Memoirs", p. 35.
17. Ibid. MG 13 WO 17, vol. 1542, pp. 91, 92, 95.
18. Ibid. RG9 IB1, vol. 25. Kerby's letters are dated 17 and 20 Apr. 1838. Maitland replied on 29 Apr. 1838.

Notes to Chapter 9

1. Cruikshank, *Kerby Memoir*, p. 187.
2. Colin Read, "The Short Hills Raid of June, 1838, and its aftermath", *Ontario History*, vol. 68, no. 3 (1976) p. 95.
3. The Army List, 1837 and 1838. The list shows Townshend as a major in the British Army.
4. Cruikshank, *Kerby Memoir*, p. 204.
5. Read, "Short Hills Raid", pp. 109-110.
6. E.A. Cruikshank, "The Insurrection in the Short Hills in 1838", *Ontario Historical Society Papers and Records*, vol.8 (1907) p. 9.
7. Sanderson, *Arthur Papers*, vol. 1, no. 208, Arthur to Colborne, 17 June 1838; no. 217, Colborne to Arthur, 25 June 1838.
8. Barthorp, *British Military Uniforms*, p. 150.
9. Guillet, *The Lives*, p. 106.
10. Cruikshank, "Insurrection", p. 10.
11. Guillet, *The Lives*, p. 107.
12. Cruikshank, *Kerby Memoir*, p. 216.
13. Read, *The Rising*, p. 138.; E. W.A. Cruikshank, "A Twice Told Tale. (The Insurrection in the Short Hills in 1838)." *Ontario Historical Society Papers and Records*, vol. 23 (1926) p. 182

14. Guillet, *The Lives*, p. 112.
15. Cruikshank, *Kerby Memoir*, p. 219.
16. Sanderson, *Arthur Papers*, vol. 1, no. 208, Arthur to Colborne, 17 June 1838.
17. Ibid., no. 238, Arthur to MacNab, 5 July 1838.
18. Cruikshank, *Kerby Memoir*, p. 223.

Notes to Chapter 10

1. George F.G. Stanley, *Canada's Soldiers* (Toronto, 1974) pp. 179-181.
2. Sanderson, *Arthur Papers* , vol. 1, no. 217, Colborne to Arthur, 25 June 1838.
3. Ibid. no. 338, Arthur to Glenelg, 29 Sept. 1838.
4. Cruikshank, *Kerby Memoir* , p. 222.
5. PAC RG9 IB1, vol. 25, Carthew to Office of the Adjutant- General of Militia, 17 Feb. 1838.
6. Read, *The Rising* , p. 150,
7. Guillet, *The Lives*, pp. 116-118.
8. Sanderson, *Arthur Papers*, vol. 1, nos. 286, 336.
9. Barthorp, *British Military Uniforms*, p. 150.
10. Sanderson, *Arthur Papers*, vol. 1, nos. 280, 286.
11. Read, "The Short Hills Raid", pp. 109-112; O.A. Kinchen, *The Rise and Fall of the Patriot Hunters* (New York, 1956), pp. 33-36.
12. Guillet, *The Lives*, pp. 116-118.
13. Senior, *Redcoats and Patriotes*, p. 155.
14. Kilbourn, Firebrand, p. 226, 236.
15. Cruikshank, *Kerby Memoir*, p. 228.
16. Sanderson, *Arthur Papers*, vol. 1, no. 403, Colborne to Arthur, 29 Oct. 1838.
17. Ibid., no. 327, Arthur to Colborne, 22 Sept. 1838.
18. Ibid. no. 336, Arthur to Colborne, 28 Sept. 1838.
19. Ibid. no. 357, Arthur to Colborne, 14 Oct. 1838; no. 358, Arthur to Col. Foster, 14 Oct. 1838..
20. PAC, C042,V.451, pp.16-22, Arthur to Glenelg, 22 Oct 1838. See also pp. 209-235.
21. Ibid. no. 357, Arthur to Colborne, 14 Oct. 1838.
22. Ibid. Colborne to Arthur, 21 Oct. 1838.
23. *Toronto Almanac 1839*, Militia List, MTPL, Baldwin Room; PAC, RG9 1B1, vol. 24 for Coloured Companies and the Runchey court martial; vols. 25 and 26 for locations of incorporated and provisional battalions. See also *Upper Canada Gazette*, 24 Oct., 8, 15 Nov. for militia general orders.
24. Sanderson, *Arthur Papers*, vol. 1, no. 421; no. 422, Report of Lieut. T.W.

Jones.

25. Senior, *Redcoats and Patriotes*, p. 187.

Notes to Chapter 11

1. Guillet, *The Lives*, Appendix N, pp. 284-285; Ella Pipping, *Soldier of Fortune* (Toronto, 1971) pp. 21-33.
2. *Brockville Recorder*, 6 Dec. 1838; PAC, C042, vol. 451, pp.545-52. Oath of Anthony Flood, 21 Nov. 1838; vol. 451, pp. 405-6, List of Papers taken from Daniel George; vol. 452, p. 351, Testimony of Orlan Blogit and p. 358, Testimony of Levi Chipman.
3. *Brockville Recorder*, 6 Dec. 1838; PAC, RG5A1, vol. 212, pp. 116625-635, Captain Williams Sandom to Major Goldie, 24 Dec. 1838; PAC, C042, vol. 451, pp. 387-422, Captain Williams Sandom to Sir George Arthur, 14 Nov. 1838; vol 451, pp. 545-52, Oath of Anthony Flood, 21 Nov. 1838; vol.452, pp. 373-78, Statement of Hely Chamberlain.
4. *Brockville Recorder* 15 Nov., 6 Dec. 1838; PAC, RG5A1, vol. 215, pp. 117881-911, Report on Patriot Activities; PAC, C042, vol. 451, pp. 553-62, Lieut. W. Newton Fowell to Capt. Williams Sandom, 12 Nov. 1838; vol 452, pp.25-37, Testimony of Ensign Edwin Smith; pp.360-61, Testimony of Willian Denis; pp. 362-63, Testimony of Charles Woodruff; *The Patriot s' War, 1837,* a translation of part of *"Geschichte de Deustchen in Syracuse and Onondaga County..."* (1897).
5. PAC, Gowan "Memoirs", pp. 45-6; *Brockville Recorder*, 15 Nov. 1838.
6. *Brockville Recorder,* 15 Nov., 22 Nov., 6 Dec. 1838; PAC, vol. 451, pp. 553-62, Lieut. Fowell to Capt. Sandom, 12 Nov. 1838; vol. 452, pp. 25-37, Testimony of Edwin Smith, Statement of von Schoultz; pp. 362-3, Testimony of Charles Woodruff.
7. *Brockville Recorder* , 22 Nov. 1838 (from the "Ogdensburg Times & Advocate"); Captain Daniel D. Heustis, *Narrative of the Adventures and Sufferings of Captain Daniel D. Heustis...* (Boston, 1847) p. 44; K.F. Scott, *Prescott's Famous Battle of the Windmill, November 13-18, 1838* (Prescott, 1970), p. 14; Pipping, *Soldier of Fortune*, pp. 138-39.
8. *Brockville Recorder*, 15 Nov., 6 Dec. 1838; PAC C042, vol. 451, pp. 553-62, Lieut. Fowell to Capt. Sandom, 12 Nov. 1838; vol. 452, pp. 358-59, Testimony of Levi Chipman.
9. *Brockville Recorder*, 6 Dec., 13 Dec. 1838; PAC, C042, vol. 452, pp. 25-32, Testimony of Edwin Smith, Statement of von Schoultz; pp.

363-65, Testimony of Orlan Blogit; PAC, RG1E3, vol. 42, p. 233, L.P. Sherwood to Arthur, 10 Dec. 1838.
10. *Brockville Recorder,* 22 Nov. 1838 (quoting *Sentinel*, Prescott, 17 Nov. 1838); PAC C042, vol. 451, pp. 478-87, Col. Plomer Young to Col. Halkett, 14 Nov. 1838; pp. 387-422 Capt. Sandom to Arthur, 14 Nov. 1838; Heustis, *Narrative*, pp. 66-67; Scott, *Windmill*, p. 19.
11. *Brockville Recorder,* 22 Nov. 1838 (quoting *Sentinel*, Prescott, 17 Nov. 1838), 6 Dec. 1838; PAC, C042, vol. 451, pp. 478-87, Col. Young to Col. Halkett, 14 Nov. 1838; pp. 478-87, Col. Henry Dundas to Arthur, 15 Nov. 1838; pp. 478-87, Capt. Sandom to Arthur, 14 Nov. 1838; vol. 452, p. 365, Testimony of Orlan Blogit; Guillet, *Lives*, p. 137; Kinchen, *The Rise*, p. 73
12. PAC, C042, vol. 451, pp. 556-58, Capt. Sandom to Arthur, 24 Nov. 1838; D.D. Heustis, *Narrative*, p. 53; Guillet, *Lives*, p. 137; Kinchen, *The Rise*, p. 76; Scott, *Windmill*, p. 30.
13. PAC, CO42, vol. 451, pp.478-87, Col. Henry Dundas to Arthur, 18 Nov. 1838.
14. *Brockville Recorder,* 22 Nov. 1838 (quoting *Sentinel*, Prescott, 17 Nov. 1838); PAC, C042, vol. 451, pp. 478-87. Dundas to Arthur, 18 Nov. 1838; pp. 478-87, Sandom to Arthur, 18 Nov. 1838; vol. 452, pp. 25-31, Statement of von Schoultz; PAC, RG5 A1, Vol. 215, pp. 117881-911, Report on Patriot Activities; Guillet, *Lives*, pp. 139-40.
15. George F.G. Stanley, "Invasion: 1838", *Ontario History*, vol. 54, no. 4 (December 1962) pp. 245-246.
16. Verna Ross McGiffin, *Pakenham: Ottawa Valley Village 1825-1860* (Pakenham, Ontario 1953) pp. 100-102.
17. Cruikshank, *Kerby Memoir*, p. 237.
18. Guillet, *The Lives*, pp. 160-161.

Notes to Chapter 12

1. PAC, CO42, vol. 451, p. 289, Arthur to Glenelg, 14 Nov. 1838; Sanderson, *Arthur Papers,* vol. 1, # 481, Arthur to Colborne, 21 Nov. 1838.
2. PAC, RG9 1B1, Court Martial 10 June 1838; also 13 June 1838; Sanderson, *Arthur Papers*, vol. 1, # 455, C.C. Domville to Knowles, 15 Nov. 1838; # 503, Arthur to Prince, 25 Nov. 1838; PAC C042, vol. 451, p. 521, Richard Airey to Arthur, 17 Nov. 1838; Cruikshank, *Kerby Memoirs*, pp. 231-32.
3. Barthorp, *British Military Uniforms*, p. 150.
4. Sanderson, *Arthur Papers*, vol. 1, # 579, Arthur to Colborne, 18 Dec.

1838.

5. Sanderson, *Arthur Papers*, vol. 1, # 518, Arthur to Col. Chichester, 2 Dec. 1838; vol. 2, # 611, Arthur to Hamilton, 2 Jan. 1839.

6. Guillet, *The Lives*, p. 144.

7. PAC WO 3708, p. 241 shows Sparke as adjutant and WO 3694 pp. 20 and 23 show Bell as captain; Douglas, *John Prince*, p. 28; Sanderson, *Arthur Papers*, vol. 1, no. 592, Arthur to Colborne, 24 Dec. 1838; R. Alan Douglas " The Battle of Windsor", *Ontario History*, vol.61, 1969, pp.141-142

8. Sanderson, *Arthur Papers*, vol. 1. no. 590, Arthur to Lord Fitzroy Somerset, 20 Dec. 1838; Douglas, "The Battle of Windsor", pp. 143-145.

9. "Diary of a Soldier in the [34th] Regiment." MTPL, Baldwin Room, p. 6. The diary is unsigned, but the contents show that an officer was the author. The quotation is from a transcript.

10. Sanderson, *Arthur Papers*, vol. 1, no. 591, Arthur to Col. Airey, 20 Dec. 1838.

11. RGI E3, vol. 42, pp. 235-236, L.P. Sherwood to Arthur, 10 Dec.1838.

12. Pipping, *Soldier of Fortune*, p. 139.

13. Guillet, *The Lives*, p. 288.

14. Ibid. p. 288.

15. PAC, RG9 lB3, vol. 10, Militia General Order, 27 Nov. 1838.

16. Sanderson, *Arthur Papers*, vol. 1, no. 461, A.G. Spearman to Arthur, 16 Nov. 1838, Treasury Chambers, London.

17. Ibid. vol. 2, no. 991, Pay and Allowances of one Troop of Cavalry (Major Magrath's) in Upper Canada one day; PAC RG9 lB3, vol. 18, Militia General Order 13 Apr. 1839.

18. Sanderson, *Arthur Papers*, vol. 2, nos. 788, 791, May 1839; Brockville *Recorder*, 23 May 1839 "Customs House Seizure", 30 May and 6 June, reports on Arthur's visit.

19. Leavitt, *Leeds and Grenville*, p. 52.

20. Guillet, *The Lives*, pp. 232-233.

21. Ibid. p. 161.

22. Sanderson, *Arthur Papers*, vol. 2, no. 866, p. 212, Arthur to Colborne, 19 Aug. 1839; Guillet, *The Lives*, p. 175, fn. 18.

23. Ibid., p. 207.

24. Sanderson, *Arthur Papers*, vol. 2, no. 996, p. 326.

Notes to Chapter 13

1. Sanderson, Arthur Papers, vol. 2, no. 1178,15 Feb. 1838.

2. Ibid. nos. 1268, 1280, 1289, 1290 p. 30, 8 to 14 Apr. 1840.

3. PRO, London, WOl, vol. 536, Arthur to Thomson, 15 Feb. !840.

4. Sanderson, Arthur Papers, vol. 2, no. 1207, Return.

5. Ibid. no. 1217, Arthur to Sir R.D. Jackson, 7 Mar. !840.

6. PAC, RG9 lB3, vol. 10, Militia General Order 16 Apr. 1840.

7. Cruikshank, *Kerby Memoir*, p. 253.

8. Sanderson, Arthur Papers, vol. 3, no. 1453, Arthur to Eden 24 Aug. 1840; no. 1462, Arthur to Russell, 2 Sept. 1840.

9. Stanley, *Canada's Soldiers*, pp. 207-208; J. Mackay Hitsman, *Safeguarding Canada 1763-1871* (Toronto I968) p. 141; PAC RG8 C Series C1194, General Order, 28 Sept. 1840.

10. Sanderson, *Arthur Papers*, vol. 3, nos. 1550, 1554, 1558, Nov. 1840.

11. Hitsman, *Safeguarding Canada*, p. 142.

12. Sanderson, *Arthur Papers*, vol. 3, nos. 1852, 1853, 1854, 1855, Mar. 1841.

13. PAC, Military Series C59, p. 375, Amos Thorne to Colley Foster, 13 Sept. 1841.

14. Hill, *Freedom Seekers*, p. 123; Hitsman, *Safeguarding Canada*, p. 145.

15. Guillet, *The Lives*, p. 231.

16. Douglas, *John Prince*, p. 102, item 275, 28 Feb. 1849; Kilbourn, *Firebrand*, pp. 241, 243.

17. Read and Stagg, *Rebellion*, p. xcix.

18. PAC, MCl3 WO17, vol. 1541, p. 149; vol. 1558, p. 4, Returns 1 Oct. 1837 and 1 Jan. 1854.

Appendix A
British Troops in Upper Canada 1837-1839

Full Name	Colour of Facings	Full Name	Colour of Facings
1st (King's) Dragoons Guards	blue	73rd Reg't of Foot	dark green
15th (York East Riding) Reg't of Foot	yellow	83rd Reg't of Foot	yellow
24th (Warwickshire Reg't of Foot)	green	85th (Bucks Volunteers) (King's Lt. Inf.) Reg't of Foot	blue
32nd (Cornwall) Reg't of Foot	white	93rd (Highland) Reg't of Foot [Gov't tartan & plaid]	yellow
34th (Cumberland) Reg't of Foot	yellow	Royal Engineers	blue velvet
43rd (Monmouthshire Lt Inf.) Reg't of Foot	white	Royal Sappers & Miners	blue
65th (2nd Yorkshire North Riding) Reg't of Foot	white	Royal Artillery [blue coatees]	red
71st (Highland Lt. Inf.) [Mackenzie tartan trews]	buff	Royal Marines	blue

Source: PAC MG I3 WO 17, vols. 1541, 1542, I543; *The Army List 1838.*

Appendix B
Independent Companies Established by December 1838

I: (Source: *The Toronto Almanac and Royal Calendar of Upper Canada.For the Year 1839*. Palladium Office, York Street,Part II)

Name	Commander
Amherst Island Independent Company	Capt. John S. Cummins
River St. Clair (Amherstburg)	Capt. J. Elliot
Belleville Independent Company Capt.	J. Warren
(attached to the 4th incorporated regiment)	
Independent Company at Bond Head	Capt. J. Dewson
Brockville Independent Artillery	Capt. John Bland
Company of Militia	
Brockville Independent Company	Capt. Robert Edmonston
Brockville Volunteer Troop	Capt. Robert Harvey
Cayuga Independent Company	Capt. R. Martin
Coloured Corps Chatham (2 companies)	Capt. George Muttlebury
	Capt. J.B. Ferrior (or Perrier)
Cornwall Artillery Company	Capt. T.H. Pringle
Farrell's Volunteer Company	Capt. A.P. Farrell
Independent Company of Militia	Capt. John McEwen
(Gananoque)	
Hastings Independent Company of Militia	Capt. J. Baxter
1st Kingston Independent Company of	Capt. C. Armstrong
Militia	
2nd Kingston Independent Company	Capt. Robert Jackson
of Militia	
Kingston Independent Company	Capt. Cameron
Magrath's Troop of Volunteer Cavalry	Capt. Thomas Magrath
(Toronto Township)	
Newcastle Independent Company	Capt. W. Beamish
Niagara Artillery Company	Capt. D. Thompson
Niagara Frontier Artillery Company	Capt. J. Baw

Name	Commander
1st Coloured Corps Niagara Frontier	Major Richard P. Webbe,
(2 companies)	Capt. Joseph B. Clench,
	Capt. A.C. Hamilton
Thompson's Volunteer Company	Capt. J. Thompson
1st Toronto Artillery	Major. Thomas Carfrae
(attached to 1st East York Regiment)	
2nd Toronto Artillery	Capt. W. Stennet
(attached to to 1st West York Regiment)	
1st Volunteer Company River Trent	Capt. W. Robertson
1st Independent Company (Walpole)	Capt. E. Evans
2nd Independent Company (Walpole)	Capt. J. Aikens
Whitby Independent Company	Capt. A. Macdonnell
Whitby Volunteers	Capt. G.H. Low
Woodstock Volunteers	Capt. R. Riddele

II: (Source: PAC RG9 lBl, vols. 24-25; lB2, vol. 17)

Name	Commander
Bytown Loyal Volunteers	Capt. George Williams Baker
Cobourg Rifle Company	Capt. Richard Chatterton
Lloydtown Independent Company	Capt. S. Tyrwhitt
Queen's Hussars (St. Catharines)	Capt. Rolland Macdonald
Queen's Light Dragoons (Toronto)	Capt. Robert Coates
Royal Essex Cavalry	Capt. Duncan Grant
Toronto City Guards (2 companies)	Major George Gurnett
Welby's Troop of Cavalry (Brantford)	Major Thomas Welby

Appendix C
The Main Events of the 1837 Rebellion Era

1834 27 March. York becomes City of Toronto; Mackenzie, already in assembly, becomes its first mayor.

October. Reformers win provincial election; Reformer Marshall Spring Bidwell is speaker of assembly.

1835 Autumn Lt. Gov. Colborne transfers to Lower Canada as commander of forces in both Canadas.

1836 23 January. Lt. Gov. Sir Francis Bond Head arrives in Toronto, appoints Reformers Baldwin, Rolph, Dunn to executive council.

4 March. Baldwin, Rolph, Dunn resign.

20 April. Head prorogues assembly.

July. Rowdy, corrupt election; Tories win a majority. Mackenzie, Bidwell lose their seats.

Autumn. Bad harvest causes rural unrest.

1837 Winter. Head refuses to appoint Bidwell a judge; Orangemen disrupt Reformers' meetings.

June-September. Mackenzie addresses meetings in townships north and west of Toronto.

31 July. Mackenzie's central committee adopts a Declaration of Independence.

September. Head resigns, awaits the arrival of a successor.

October. Head sends 24th Regiment to Lower Canada to suppress rebels; 4,000 to 6,000 small arms at Toronto's City Hall guarded by two constables; Bonnycastle goes to Kingston to command the militia.

November Mackenzie publishes constitution on the American model; Thomas Cubitt takes one company of Royal Artillery from Quebec City to Kingston.

18 November. Mackenzie decides on coup d'état for 7 December.

2 December. Rolph advances date of coup to 4 December, causes confusion.

7 December. Rebels dispersed on Yonge Street near Montgomery's Tavern, fail to capture Toronto.

11 December. Mackenzie reaches Buffalo.

8-13 December. Duncombe gathers rebels at Scotland, Oakland Township southwest of Brantford.

13 December. Mackenzie sets up provisional government on Navy Island, in the Niagara River.

14 December. Duncombe's followers disperse as MacNab's militia approaches.

28-30 December. Head approves raising of six regiments of incorporated militia.

29 December. Burning of U.S. steamer *Caroline* by loyal Canadians under Andrew Drew.

1838 January. The 24th Regiment returns; Colborne sends a further reinforcement of the 32nd Regiment and two companies of the 83rd to Upper Canada.

8-9 January. American "patriot" force occupies Bois Blanc Island off Amherstburg, sloop *Anne* captured by Canadian militia.

13-14 January. Mackenzie evacuates Navy Island, goes to Buffalo.

17 January. Head inspects Navy Island.

22 February. On Hickory Island (in the Thousand Islands) Mackenzie abandons plan to attack Kingston.

23 February. American republicans occupy Fighting Island, Detroit River; Canadian militia routes them by 25 February.

26 February to 3 March. Republicans occupy Pelee Island, Lake Erie; routed by regulars of 32nd and 83rd Regiments and the Essex Militia by 3 March.

23 March. Sir George Arthur arrives to succeed Head as lieutenant governor.

24 March. Head leaves for England by way of New York State.

13 April. Executions of Matthews and Lount at Toronto.

29-30 May. Burning of Canadian steamer *Sir Robert Peel* by "Pirate" Bill Johnston in Thousand Islands.

June. The 34th Regiment arives, followed shortly by three companies of the 85th.

10-21 June. Short Hills raid, attack on St. Johns, in Pelham Township.

June. Republicans cross St. Clair River twice to loot; U.S. sloop loots Goderich. Lord Durham arrives in Quebec City as governor general.

July. The 43rd Regiment leaves Lower Canada for Niagara and Colborne follows with two companies of King's Dragoon Guards and one company of Royal Artillery.

11 July. Durham reaches Kingston to begin a week-long visit to Upper Canada.

17 July. Durham reviews the 43rd and other regulars at Niagara, a show of force to impresss the Americans.

30 July. James Morreau is hanged at Niagara for his part in the Short Hills raid.

August. Detachment of 71st Regiment sent to Brockville to prevent quarrels by political factions.

1 November. Durham sails for England to report.

11-16 November. Battle of the Windmill near Prescott; republicans and rebels under von Schoultz defeated, many captured.

16 November. Murder of militia captain, Edgeworth Ussher, at Chippawa; battle among militiamen at Pakenham.

21 November. U.S. proclamation: Americans crossing into Canada will not be given protection.

28 November. Trials of prisoners taken at Prescott begin; John A. Macdonald advises von Schoultz, others.

December. The 73rd Regiment arrives, moves to Brantford.

4 December. Battle of Windsor; republicans and Canadian exiles cross from Detroit, are routed by John Prince and the Essex Militia.

8-22 December. Executions of Nils von Schoultz, Dorrephus Abbey, Daniel George, Martin Woodruff, Joel Peeler, Sylvanus Sweet at Kingston.

Late December. Remaining companies of the 85th Regiment, all of the 93rd, and three companies of the 65th arrive in Upper Canada.

1839 4 January to 11 February. Executions of Christopher Buckley, Sylvester Lawton, Russell Phelps, Duncan Anderson, Leman Leach at Kingston.

7 January to 6 February. Executions of Hiram Lynn, Daniel Bedford, Albert Clark, Cornelius Cunningham, Joshua Doan, Amos Perley at London.

March. Durham's report reaches the Canadas.

April. Numerous incidents; British and American ships fire on each other in the St. Lawrence; much tension.

10 June. Americans sentence Mackenzie to eighteen months in jail at Canandaigua, New York.

12 July. Orange parade cancelled in Cobourg, as a concession to Reformers.

17 July. Rebel-republican plan to rob and murder in Cobourg foiled.

September. Canadian, American prisoners gathered at Kingston, sent by Rideau Canal to Quebec; some ninety are transported to penal servitude in Van Diemen's Land (Tasmania).

13 September. Anglican church in Chippawa burnt.

1840 April. Top blown off Brock Monument, Queenston, by republicans.

10 May. Mackenzie released from jail in New York State.

1841 September. Attempt to blow up locks of Welland Canal foiled.

15 September. President John Tyler issues proclamation to suppress secret societies.

1842 10 June. Mackenzie moves his family to New York City.

1843 During the year some rebel leaders receive pardons; other rebels are granted amnesty.

1849 1 February. Mackenzie pardoned, by which time some men have returned from Van Diemen's Land, some remain, others have died there.

18 March. Mackenzie returns to Toronto, attempt made to lynch him.

25 April. Royal assent given Rebellion Losses Bill.

1850 1 May. Mackenzie brings his family to Toronto.

1851 April. Mackenzie wins seat in assembly as member for Haldimand. Dies 28 August 1861.

ILLUSTRATION AND MAP CREDITS

Canadian War Museum, Canadian Museum of Civilization 58 (right).

William Constable 10(left), 14, 42(left), 46,47,57,68,80,81(right), 94,105.

Geoffrey R.D. Fryer 119

Mary Beacock Fryer 96(upper)

Nicol G.W. Kingsmill 55

Metropolitan Toronto Library 8, 9, 10(right), 11,12,13, 19, 20, 21(left), 22, 23, 24, 28, 29(left), 30, 31, 33(left), 35, 37, 38, 39, 40, 41, 43, 44, 48(right), 49, 50, 41, 53, 56, 59, 61(right), 66, 67, 69, 71, 72, 74(upper), 76, 77, 83, 84(lower), 87, 90, 92(right), 93, 96(lower), 97, 98, 99, 100, 104,106, 109, 110, 111, 114, 115, 116(right), 122, 125, 126, 127, 130, 131, 132, 133, 134, 135.

Ontario Archives 33(right), 45, 52, 60, 61(left), 74(lower), 85, 92(left), 103,108,118, 124.

Public Archives of Canada 17, 18, 21(right), 25, 26, 29(right), 32, 34, 42(right), 48(left), 58(left), 75, 78, 81(left), 82, 84(upper), 91, 95, 129.

John H. Prince 116(left).

Royal Canadian Yacht Club 88

BIBLIOGRAPHICAL NOTE

A useful secondary source was Edwin C. Guillet's book, *The Lives and Times of the Patriots*. Although his style of documentation does not meet modern academic standards, Guillet unearthed considerable contemporary material from newspapers and eyewitness versions of most of the military operations. His extensive appendices contain a wealth of detail that supplements his main text.

The official records for the period when Sir Francis Bond Head was the lieutenant governor are less satisfactory than those kept by his successor, Major-General Sir George Arthur. J.C. Dent concluded that the records for the militia had been destroyed when the Parliament Building in Montreal was burnt in 1849. However, two valuable collections are extant. A large quantity of militia lists was forwarded to the War Office in London and preserved in he Public Archives of Canada as MG13 WO13. These are not necessarily an accurate reflection of who was active in late 1837 and early 1838. More useful for this period is a collection of records for the Upper Canadian Militia that remained in the province. The originals are in the Public Archives of Canada and identified as Record Group 9 (RG9). These are RG9 1B1, Correspondence of the Adjutant-General's Office, Upper Canada; RG9 1B2, Daily and Weekly State of the Incorporated Militia: and RG9 1B3, Militia General Orders. RG9 1B3 is a small collection, and more Militia General Orders were published in the Upper Canada Gazette than are found in the Archives.

The most extensive printed primary source is *The Arthur Papers*, three volumes which were edited by Charles R. Sanderson for the Toronto Public Library in 1957. As could be expected of an experienced military commander, Sir George Arthur kept careful records during his term in office. The papers of Lieutenant-General Sir John Colborne, Arthur's superior officer, were marginally useful, but these relate more to Lower Canada, where Colborne was in direct command. The Mackenzie-Lindsey Papers, in the Ontario Archives, form the largest collection on the rebellions in Upper Canada. While they contain considerable information about the rebel side, they are less specific about the military who opposed Mackenzie.

The War Office records were illuminating for the regular troops. Three important returns — or lists — are on microfilm in the Public Archives of Canada as MG13 WO17. The returns show the numbers and distribution of the professional soldiers by regiments. *The Army List* yielded the correct ranks for the regular officers, details not often found in contemporary reports. Many officers were given higher local ranks, which were sometimes a step towards promotion in the field.

A valuable secondary reference was Brigadier-General Ernest Alexander Cruikshank's memoir on the Honourable James Kerby, a militia commander on the Niagara frontier. In the fashion of historians early in this century, Cruikshank did not document his book, but most of his material was drawn from Record Group 9. The memoir is useful for other parts of the province, for Cruikshank took a very broad approach. He brought in events that were occurring elsewhere, not just in the Niagara area. Like Cruikshank, Colin Read made use of Record Group 9 in describing the military operations in his book, *The Rising in Western Upper Canada 1837-8*.

The correspondence between militia officers and the Adjutant-General's Office in RG9 1B1 revealed where each regimental headquarters was located, and for what length of time, for both the incorporated and the sedentary militia units. *The Toronto Almanac 1839* included a list of the officers in the militia by regiment at the close of 1838, and gave the names of the towns and townships from which each regiment was drawn. *The Arthur Papers* had information on the changes that took place after this list was compiled.

Contemporary accounts were written by James FitzGibbon and Sir Richard Bonnycastle. While biased in his own favour, FitzGibbon's two narratives present a lively picture of the rebellion on Yonge Street. Bonnycastle comes to life as a genial man who enjoyed reciting anecdotes in his description of the preparations for the defence of Kingston.

The Blandford Press, of Poole, Dorset, England, specializes in British military history, and two recent books provided background. Michael Barthorp's book on uniforms has descriptions of the regimentals worn by regular troops in the 1830s, and the colours of the facings listed correspond to those in The Army List. Frederick Myatt's book on the British infantry has a concise account of the reorganization of the British army in 1825.

The documents in Read and Stagg's book, *The Rebellion of 1837*, and many of the county histories, yielded information on how the rebellions affected towns, villages and townships. Some were settings for the risings and raids. Others were remote, and the main activity was the mustering of the militia units. In these areas the men were often sent home before they could march because the emergency came to an end.

Every effort was made to find the full names of the participants and something about them. Very little is known about some of the men who played prominent roles, while a great deal is known about others. For example, R. Alan Douglas wrote a book about John Prince, who was active in the Windsor-Sandwich area. On the other hand almost nothing was found about Joseph Hill, who commanded incorporated militia. The papers of the Magrath family of Erindale are in the Peel Region Museum, but these reveal nothing about the services of Thomas Magrath's dragoon troop that featured so largely in the rebellions and the later republican raids.

The contemporary versions of the incidents, large and small, show variations. Where certain details conflicted, what seemed to be the most logical interpretation of events was used. Confusion was evident over the location of Gallows Hill, whether it was south of St. Clair Avenue, or farther north on the rise above Mount Pleasant Cemetery. In his book *Toronto of Old*, Henry Scadding's description (on pages 307-309) of Yonge Street north of Yorkville Avenue, places Gallows Hill south of Deer Park village, which grew up around the St. Clair-Yonge intersection. The hill was not named because it was a place of execution, but for a tree that had fallen across a narrow excavation that had been cut to make the road less steep. The tree reminded people of the arm of a scaffold. The name had its effect on later residents. One lady of an old Deer park family told her grandson that she vividly recalled the days when ropes still dangled from the old scaffold. Memory plays odd tricks.

BIBLIOGRAPHY

Original Sources

Manuscript

Militia Records

Public Archives of Canada:
 RG9 1B1, Correspondence of the Adjutant-General's Office, Upper Canada.
 RG9 1B2, Daily and Weekly State of the Incorporated Militia.
 RG9 1B3, Militia General Orders.
 MG13 WO13, Muster Books and Pay Lists, Militia and Volunteers, Upper and Lower Canadian Militia, vols. 3673-3716 for the years 1837-1842.
Ontario Archives:
 Militia lists for individual companies.

Regular Regiments

Public Archives of Canada:
 MG13 WO17, vol. 1541 (1 October 1837), 1542 (1 June 1838), 1543 (1 March 1839), 1558 (1 January 1854).
 RG8 Series C, British Military and Naval Records.

Public Record Office, London:
 WO1, vols. 522, 536.

Other Records

Colborne Papers, Public Archives of Canada, MG24 A40.
Diary 1838-40 of a Soldier in the [34th] Regiment, by an anonymous officer. Metropolitan Toronto Public Library, Baldwin Room.
Foster Papers (Colonel Colley Foster), Ontario Archives.
Gowan Memoirs. Public Archives of Canada, in Ferguson Papers, MG27 IE30, vol. 5, pp. 1-60.
Mackenzie-Lindsey Papers, Ontario Archives.
Upper Canada Sundries, Public Archives of Canada RG5 A1 (on microfilm in the Ontario Archives).

Printed Sources

Army List, The. A List of General and Field Officers, Whitehall 1837, 1838.
Bonnycastle, Sir Richard H. *Canada as it Was, Is, and May Be*. London 1852, 2 vols.
———. *The Canadas in 1841*. Reprint, New York 1908, 2 vols.
Brockville *Recorder*. Issues for November, December 1838, May 1839, *Recorder and Times* office, Brockville.
FitzGibbon, James. *An Appeal to the People of the Late Province of Upper Canada*. Montreal, 24 May 1847.
———. *Narrative on the Occurrences in Toronto in December 1837*. Toronto, 13 December 1837.
Kingston Chronicle and Gazette. Issues for late November and December 1838.
Sanderson, Charles R., ed. *The Arthur Papers*, 3 vols., Toronto Public Library 1957.
Toronto Almanac 1839. Published by Palladium, Charles Fothergill, proprietor, Metropolitan Toronto Public Library, Baldwin Room.
Upper Canada Gazette 1837-1838, newspaper collection in the Ontario Archives.

Secondary Sources

Barthorp, Michael. *British Infantry Uniforms Since 1660*.Blandford Press, Poole, Dorset, England 1982.

Berchem, F.R. *The Yonge Street Story 1793-1860*. Toronto 1977.

Bonis, Robert P., ed. *A History of Scarborough*. Scarborough 1968.

Carter, J. Smyth. *The Story of Dundas*. Iroquois 1905. Reprint 1973.

Champion, Isabel, ed. *Markham 1795-1906*. Markham District Historical Museum 1979.

Craig, Gerald M. *Upper Canada: The Formative Years 1784-1841*. Toronto 1963.

Cruikshank, E.A. *A Memoir of the Honourable James Kerby, His Life and Letters*. Welland County Historical Society Papers and Records, vol. 4, Welland 1931.

——."The Insurrection in the Short Hills in 1838." *Ontario Historical Society Papers and Records*, vol. 8 1907.

——.*The Thirteenth Battalion of Infantry*. Hamilton 1899.

Dent, John Charles. *The Upper Canadian Rebellion*. 2 vols., Toronto 1885.

Douglas, R. Alan. *John Prince 1796-1870*. Champlain Society, Ontario Series No. 11, Toronto 1980.

Dunham, Aileen. *Political Unrest in Upper Canada, 1815-1836*. Toronto 1963, Reprint 10, The Carleton Library.

Fortesque, Sir John William. *A History of the British Army*. vol. 9, 1815-1838. London 1923.

Fordyce, Lieut. A.,M. *The Oxford Rifles*. Reprinted from the *Daily Sentinel-Review*, Woodstock, March 1926.

Green, Ernest. "Upper Canada's Black Defenders."*Ontario Historical Society Papers and Records,* vol. 27 (1931).

Guillet, Edwin C. *The Lives and Times of the Patriots*. Toronto 1938 and 1963.

Hamil, Fred Coyne. *The Valley of the Lower Thames*. Toronto 1951.

Hart, Patricia W. *Pioneering in North York*. Toronto 1968.

Hill, Daniel G. *The Freedom Seekers: Blacks in Early Canada*. Agincourt, Ontario 1981.

Hitsman, J. Mackay. *Safeguarding Canada 1763-1871*. Toronto 1968.

——. *The Incredible War of 1912*. Toronto 1965.

Howard, Richard B. *Colborne's Legacy: Upper Canada College 1829-1979*. Toronto 1979.

Hunter, Andrew F. *The History of Simcoe County*. 2 parts. The Historical Society of Simcoe County, Barrie 1948; originally published by the author in 1909.

Jackman, Sydney W. *Galloping Head: the Life of the Right Honourable Sir Francis Bond Head, Bart., P.C., 1793-1875 Late Lieutenant-Governor of Upper Canada*. London 1958.

Johnson, Leo A. *History of Guelph 1827-1927*. Guelph Historical Society, Guelph 1977.

Johnson, J.K. "Sir James Gowan, Sir John A. Macdonald and the Rebellion of 1837." *Ontario History,* vol. 60 (1968).

——1837-1838." *Ontario History*, vol. 64 (1972).

Johnston, Charles M. *Brant County: a History 1784-1945*. Toronto 1967.

Johnston, William. *History of Perth County 1825-1902*. Stratford 1903, reprint 1976.

Kilbourn, William. *The Firebrand: William Lyon Mackenzie and the Rebellion in Upper Canada*. Toronto 1956.

Landon, Fred. *An Exile From Canada*. Toronto 1960.

——. *Western Ontario and the American Frontier*. Toronto 1941.

Leavitt, Thad. W.H. *History of Leeds and Grenville Ontario From 1749 to 1879*. Brockville 1879.

Lee, David. *Battle of the Windmill, 1838*. National Historic Parks and Sites Branch, Parks Canada, History and Archaeology. Publication no. 8.

Lindsey, Charles. *The Life and Times of William Lyon Mackenzie*. 2 vols., Toronto 1862.

Longley, R.S. "Emigration and the Crisis of 1837 in Uppr Canada. *Canadian Historical Review*. vol. 17 (1936).

Macpherson, K.R. "A List of Vessels Employed on British Service on the Great Lakes 1755-1857." *Ontario History*, vol. 55 (1963).

Martyn, J.P. "The Patriot Invasion of Pelee Island." *Ontario History*. vol. 56 (Sept. 1964).

Mathews, Hazel C. *Oakville and the Sixteen*. Champlain Society, Toronto 1953.

McGiffin, Verna Ross. *Pakenham: Ottawa Valley Village 1823-1860*. Pakenham, Ontario 1963.

McKenzie, Ruth. *James FitzGibbon Defender of Upper Canada*. Toronto 1983.

McLenan, R.R. *To the Surviving Veterans of 1837-8-9*. Alexandria, Ontario 1892 (pamphlet).

Moir, John S. "FitzGibbon's Secret Visitor."*Ontario History* vol. 48 (1956).

Muir, R. Cuthbertson. *The Early Political and Military History of Burford*. Quebec 1913.

Myatt, Frederick. *The British Infantry 1660-1945*. Blandford Press, Poole, Dorset, England 1983.

Ontario Historical Society, Edith Firth ed., *Profiles of a Province*. Toronto 1967.

Pipping, Ella. *Soldier of Fortune*. Toronto 1967 and 1971.

Read, Colin, and Stagg, Ronald J. *The Rebellion of 1837 in Upper Canada*. Champlain Society, Ontario Series No. 12. Toronto 1985.

Read, Colin. *The Rising in Western Upper Canada*, 1837-8: The Duncombe Revolt and After. Toronto 1982.

——. "The Short Hills Raid in June, 1838, and its Aftermath." *Ontario History*, vol. 68 (1976).

Robertson, H.H. *The Gore District Militia of 1821-1824-1830- 1838*. Wentworth Historical Society, Hamilton 1904.

Ryerson, Egerton. *The Story of My Life*. Toronto 1883.

Scadding, Henry. *Toronto of Old*. Originally published in 1873, reprinted in 1966, abridged and edited by F.H. Armstrong, Toronto 1966. 2nd edition, 1987

Schull, Joseph. *Rebellion: The Rising in French Canada 1837*. Toronto 1971.

Scott, James. *The Settlement of Huron County*. Toronto 1966.

Scott, K.F. *Prescott's Famous Battle of the Windmill November 13-18*. Prescott, June 1970.

Senior, Elinor Kyte. *Redcoats and Patriotes: The Rebellions in Lower Canada 1837-38*. Canadian War Museum Historical Publication No. 20, Ottawa 1985.

Stagg, Ronald J. "The Yonge Street Rebellion of 1837: An Examination of the Social Background and a Re-assessment of the Events." PhD dissertation, University of Toronto 1976.

Stanley, George F.G. "Invasion 1838." *Ontario History*, vol. 54 (December 1962). .

——. *Canada's Soldiers*. Toronto 1974.

Turner, Capt. A.T. *History of the l2th Regiment York Rangers*. Toronto, no date.

Tulchinsky, Gerald, ed. *To Preserve and Defend: Essays on Kingston in the Nineteenth Century*. Montreal and London 1976.

Upper Canada Almanac 1837. Metropolitan Toronto Public Library, Baldwin Room.

INDEX

(The rank for each individual listed is the highest attained either in the British Army, the Royal Navy, the Canadian Militia, or the Provincial Marine during the period 1837-39.)

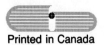

Printed in Canada